3-16-76

A NEW AGE IN THEOLOGY

A NEW AGE IN THEOLOGY

by
Claude Geffré

Translated by
**Robert Shillenn
with Francis McDonagh
and Theodore L. Westow**

PAULIST PRESS
New York / Paramus / Toronto

A Paulist Press edition, originally published as *Un Nouvel Age de la Théologie* by Les Editions de Cerf, Paris, © 1972.

Chapter 1, translated by Theodore L. Westow, appeared previously in English in *Concilium*, Vol. 46, published by Paulist Press. Chapter 3, translated by Francis McDonagh, appeared in *Concilium*, Vol. 76, published by The Seabury Press, Inc. The remaining portions of this book have been translated by Robert Shillenn.

Library of Congress
Catalog Card Number: 74-12634

ISBN: 0-8091-1844-0

Cover by Morris Berman

Published by Paulist Press
Editorial Office: 1865 Broadway, N.Y., N.Y. 10023
Business Office: 400 Sette Drive, Paramus, N.J. 07652

Printed and bound in the
United States of America

1906973

Contents

Foreword

When he asked me to introduce his short book with the alluring and provocative title *A New Age in Theology* to the reader, Father Geffré not only showed his friendly confidence in me (which is something older people especially appreciate), but he also showed that he is well aware of the problem today so feverishly debated, concerning break and continuity in the historical fabric of the faith, or understanding the faith throughout the course of history. In all areas of knowledge epistemological analysis is attaining a high degree of insight. It is discerning, through a synthesis of even progress and qualitative leaps forward, often involving breaks in continuity, a creativity which is definitely transforming methods and projects. In the history of civilizations the historian identifies re-births which are difficult to pinpoint, periods, eras as well as "new ages." By inviting me, an old man, into the dialogue, Father Geffré bears witness to the continuity of generations. At the same time he honors me by recognizing in me one who, not without some boldness and certain risks, has reacted against decay in theology and envisaged opportune breakthroughs in historical and speculative method. Perhaps it could be said that the expression *new age* is too strong for anyone who has studied the profound upheaval of the Reformation and the Renaissance and still feels its effects; but I am inclined to think that our descendants in the twenty-first century will acknowledge in our time a "reformation" and a "renaissance" more radical than those of the sixteenth century, at least in their outcome.

The very structure of theology is being called into question, precisely insofar as it is *reason* creatively at work within the faith, at a time when reason is beginning to appreciate the demands of its own autonomy. If the Church is *in* the world, ac-

1

cording to the constitutional principle set forth by Vatican Council II, the Gospel is *in* history: *historical* reason is the nerve of this "new theology." Here is its anatomy and I am extremely pleased with the diagnosis.

Among so many reflections and suggestions, I would readily settle on the historical method as a common denominator of the problems and innovations I have encountered, recognized, and set forth, although today I sometimes feel they are at an impasse. Some clear memories come back to mind, minor episodes in the journey of theology from the Modernist crisis to its final leap before liquidation, when the "new theology" was denounced from on high in 1946-1950 in the encyclical *Humani Generis.*

When I entered the race as an historian of Christian doctrine, I applied, as a good professional in my field, the historical method to the critical analysis of the literary and cultural contexts of dogmatic statements and theological elaborations, including those of Saint Thomas Aquinas. The work was carried out in the cast of the famous manifesto of Father Lagrange. The *historical method* (1902) as applied to Scripture was highly suspect both then and now to official and unofficial authorities who no more consented to the historicity of Saint Thomas' theology than to that of the dogmas of the faith. The ingenuous ignorance of people like Billot and Garigou-Lagrange show both the extent of this improbable obstruction and the reason for it. But, quite early, I got beyond the stage in which history was still considered extrinsic, and I recognized that historicity is an intrinsic dimension of the Word of God in the concrete event of revelation fulfilled in Jesus Christ. See pages 14-20, where note is taken of the failure of the objectivist rationalism of an "apologetics" incapable of perceiving the radicality of Modernism and pages 74-78 on that twofold dimension. The object of theology is the *history of salvation* and within that history, God— the God of Jesus Christ—and not the Pure Act of Aristotle or the God of the Enlightenment and Joseph II of Austria.

Two breaking points: the rejection of the threefold division according to which, for three centuries following the Counter-Reformation, theology was set up, and secondly the elimination of the positive and speculative theology dualism which, right from when I began resorting to it, damaged my *intellectus fidei.* When I publicly outlined my proposal at the Saulchoir, Roman theologians crossed out my text with big black lines; "scorn for and destruction of Scholastic theology," declared one high-ranking personality (who after Vatican II took up my proposal as his own).

History: past, present, future. Here all the dimensions of the Word of God are recovered. The greatest, perhaps the most notable problem is presence: God speaks today. That is the hermeneutical problem, the nerve center for what is now going on. When, about forty years ago, we were re-introducing pastoral theology as a living substance, in opposition to the dualism surviving from the controversies of the last Council, it was a preliminary episode of the present recasting of theology. I daresay, even as just an archaeological remark, that we again find in new categories the classic formulation of the thirteenth century, then defined as comprising three stages: *lectio, disputatio, predicatio:* "exegesis, theology, pastoral application," as a colleague of Father Geffré's recently stated (*Nouvelle Revue Theologique,* 1966, pp. 3-13, 132-148). The master of theology, it used to be said, should devote himself among his other duties to preaching: applied theology. The world is the place for the Word of God, without taking away from its transcendence or its gratuity. The theologian as a man among men ought to take on, along with his scientific function, a prophetic function. This word, although unfortunately often debased, seizes us in the deepest reaches of our faith in its act of understanding.

If I have given in to personal reminiscences, over and above what is proper, it is because I welcome Father Geffré's fraternal invitation to give my account of the period before Vatican II and the post-conciliar age with the satisfaction of an old fellow for young people who still listen to him.

M.-D. Chenu

Preface

It surely would be rash to speak of a *kairos* or "favorable time" for theology in the way that Hegel believed that he could hail a *kairos* for philosophy. But there are "ages" in theology and we are in a favorable position to begin going into detail about the outlines of this "post-Vatican II" theological age. At the end of the Council, Karl Rahner wrote that "the themes that the Council leaves behind for the theology of tomorrow are not that it dealt with itself . . ." He certainly read the situation accurately. However, this famous "theology of tomorrow" should not forever remain a beautiful utopia which obscures the modest accomplishments of today.

The studies gathered into this volume all concern the current ferment in theology which gives us the right to speak of a new "age" in theology. They do not claim to paint even an incomplete picture of contemporary theological research. They aim less at providing information than at pointing out where research is converging and introducing a reflection on the most significant changes in theology since Vatican II. The best way to arouse the reader's attention to the true theological stakes in the various chapters of this book is by giving in the form of a foreward what are in my view the most important expressions of this current theological turning-point.

First of all, we are witnessing a certain overstepping of ecumenical boundaries. The cleavages among the various theologies are occurring much more within each denomination. It is remarkable that von Balthasar is playing the same role within Catholicism as Karl Barth did within Protestantism in his defense of the transcendental and vertical affirmations of revelation against any attempt at reconciliation between Christianity and the world (cf. Chapter 1: "Recent Developments in Fun-

5

damental Theology"). And Protestant authors such as Tillich and Pannenberg are rediscovering the importance of fundamental theology and even natural theology to insure the credibility of the Christian faith in the face of unbelieving reason (cf. Chapter 4: "From the Theologies of the Word to the Theology of History"). If I think I have been able to identify theologians of *mediation* (between faith and reason, between the Church and the world) and theologians of Christian *positivity*, it would be impossible to divide them according to their denominational allegiance. This leads me to believe that spiritualities and the practical applications by the Church can play a more important role in reshaping the face of theology than belonging to this or that Christian denomination.

This first observation leads us to secondly note a much greater *pluralism* in post-Vatican II theology. This creates a new situation for the Magisterium as well as for the teaching of theology. This pluralism is due to the plurality of philosophies and current experiences of existence. But it is also due to plurality of the forms of Christian involvement for which theology is seeking to account. Theology can no longer be satisfied with being the justification of the teaching of the Magisterium or the transmission of already constituted knowledge. As an actualization of the Word of God, theology is only faithful to its task if the life of the Church in a given concrete situation is where it is most prominent, and if its interpretation of Christianity leads to a renewal in its practical application by Christians. It is in this perspective that the current of political theology must be understood (cf. Chapter 5: "The Political Dimension of Christian Hope"). But as I point out, theology should not on this account give up its universal import for every intelligence, believing or unbelieving, in quest of truth. Besides, any theology which would be no more the justification of the practical applications of some particular Church quickly runs the risk of turning into ideology.

Overstepping the narrowness of ecumenical boundaries, inevitable pluralism—these are not sufficient to characterize this new theological age we have entered. Several times in this volume I come back to the hermeneutical orientation of theology

(cf. Chapter 2: "Dogmatic Theology in the Hermeneutic Age").
This is not giving in to a fashion, but taking note of a new understanding of Scripture and of a new situation in theology
which is seeking to bring out the permanent significance of the
Word of God in its scriptural, dogmatic and theological forms
in terms of the historical understanding man has of himself and
of the world. The teaching of dogmatic theology cannot be confined to the serene presentation of a given guaranteed by the
Magisterium. It must aim at an interpretation of the statements
of the faith in such a way that they become something more
than mere verbal orthodoxy and really penetrate contemporary
understanding. This new awareness of the hermeneutical dimension of theology brings along with it important consequences for
the method of theology, in particular concerning the relationship between dogma and Scripture, and between dogmatic
and biblical theology (cf. Chapter 2).

But what is most important for the future of theology is
unquestionably to reflect with renewed energy, in terms of our
philosophical modernity, on the nature of *theological reason*. I
am attempting to show that although it is impossible to give up
the speculative ambition of theology and the ontological range
of its language, we are not necessarily forced to identify theological reason with metaphysical reason which is understood as
an attempt at explaining under the sign of the Logos (cf.
Chapter 3: "A Non-Metaphysical Theology"). We can never
say enough how much the current crisis in metaphysical thought
is occasioning a critical reexamination of the foundations of
speculative theology. But I personally think that we are in a favorable position to devote ourselves to a rereading of our theological tradition by *suspecting* the overly connatural association
between the God of the philosophers and the God of Judaeo-
Christian tradition.

Finally, something which characterizes this new theological
age is the desire to get out of the ghetto of a clerical theology
mainly polarized by institutional problems internal to the
Church. Theology aspires to be the place for dialogue between
the Church and the world. Theology is not only understanding
of the faith but questioning at the heart of the faith. At the

same time the theologian seeks understanding of the Word of God for today: he witnesses before God to the most radical questions of modern man. So questions about the meaning of history, about the future of man and the world, about the effectiveness of Christianity are at the root of a great many contemporary theological undertakings. You should not be surprised if I give a lot of space to Pannenberg's *theology of history*, Moltmann's *theology of hope* and Metz' *political theology* (cf. Chapters 4 and 5), as particularly significant of a new theological turning-point. It seemed to me just as important to insist on the remarkable renewal of the theology of the resurrection of Christ which is inaugurating a new balance of *theology* and *economy of salvation* and which dominates the very structure of Christology and the theology of history (cf. Chapter 6: "The Resurrection of Christ as the Center of Christian Theology").

I have refrained from speaking in Chapter 2 about *non-authoritarian* theology. This is perhaps the most appropriate term to characterize this new age of theology. It is not a matter of questioning the authority of the Word of God without which all theology crumbles. This radical dependence makes for the congenital weakness and also the greatness of scientific theology in relation to the ideal of autonomy in the other sciences. But by speaking of *non-authoritarian* theology I am referring to the freedom and daring of a theology which is striving to overcome the divorce between the faith and modern reason's rule of autonomy. It is a fact that modern intelligence does not easily accept any truth in the name of an authority, even God's. Truth should be capable of arousing conviction by the very strength of its content. Today, as yesterday, theology cannot invoke a "supernatural authority" to relieve itself of its task of insuring the credibility of Christianity confronted with inescapable demands of reason. But this will not only be done by seeking the intelligible reason for the various Christian mysteries. It will also be accomplished by demonstrating the historical foundations of Judaeo-Christian revelation.

In short, starting with different approaches, this short book is intended to show how much the Christian theology of today is seeking to move out from its cultural isolation by overcoming, in the very name of the Gospel, the false gulf between faith and modern reason, between the Church and the world, between the history of salvation and history pure and simple.

1. Recent Developments in Fundamental Theology

In contrast with the other theological disciplines, the nature of fundamental theology is still hotly debated among theologians.[1] The most common definitions today betray a definite uncertainty about the epistemology of a discipline which wants to fulfill at the same time the function of the old apologetics— i.e., that of providing a rational justification of the Christian faith—and exercise the critical function inherent in all science— i.e., that of explaining the basis and method of the science of theology.

Take, for example, the definition given in the recent French *Dictionary of Theology:* "Fundamental theology refers either to the defensive and justifying function of theology or to that sector of theology concerned with the study of the Word of God and man's acceptance of this Word."[2] According to Y. Congar, from whom this definition has been taken, one can consider fundamental theology as an integral part of theology (a treatise on the Word of God and its acceptance by man) or as a potential part (the defensive and justifying function).[3]

We might be tempted to see in this "justifying" function the most characteristic contribution of fundamental theology. While we would not want to return to the excesses that beset the apologetics of the old school, we should not reduce it either to a treatise on revelation or on the sources of theology (*loci theologici*).[4] It must always be concerned with showing forth the rational character of the act of faith. But we should add at once that Congar's definition does not explicitly mention a third function of fundamental theology—namely that of examining critically the nature and method of theology as a science, or in other words, providing theology with an epistemology and methodology.[5]

The meaning of fundamental theology is therefore somewhat variable, and this should make us beware of pinning it down to a too rigid definition as if it were once and for all perfectly clear about its object, its themes and its method. If its specific function is to explain Christianity to the human mind, one will already expect its set of subjects and even its method to develop according to the historical development of the mind. We shall thus have to allow even more room for historical relativity in the structure and practice of fundamental theology than in the other sectors of theology.

It is in this light that I would therefore like to try to interpret the recent history of fundamental theology. This is not going to be a historical sketch, however brief, of this theology from the beginning of this century.[6] But I believe that we can discern three main tendencies which followed each other chronologically, and this with a certain historical logic. We begin with the collapse of apologetics as an objective science to the benefit of a fundamental theology, the starting point of which is frankly theological and historical. From there we shall pass on to the *anthropocentric* view which inspires most modern works on fundamental theology. And this will lead us to the tendency which is beginning to take shape today and which reaches beyond objectivism and anthropocentrism to the social and political existence of modern man.

I

From Apologetics to Fundamental Theology

Historical Background

The idea of an "apology of the faith" goes back to the origins of Christianity. One can find it already in the New Testament where its charter may be recognized in 1 Peter 3, 15: "Always have your answer ready for people who ask you the reason for the hope that you all have, but give it with courtesy and respect and with a clear conscience." But it was only in the context of the 18th century's interdenominational controversies that a science of apologetics was built up in order to create a methodical approach to this vindication of the Christian faith. Today the word "apologetics" has become suspect, and we may say that the era of "handbooks of apologetics" is now closed. The term is replaced by that of fundamental theology, a term already in use in the 19th century, in order to describe the discipline which aims at justifying the foundations of our faith and therefore of our theology.

Now, it is very instructive to look at the historical causes of this apologetic inflation in Catholic theology during the last centuries, and the reasons for its decline. This bent for apologetics can only be understood in connection with the Reformation, the rationalist triumph of the Enlightenment and the cultural phenomenon of atheism.[7]

Lutheran theology used to emphasize the subjective factors —particularly the part played by the Spirit—which give the certainty of the divine origin of our faith as soon as they make the believer accept the contents of revelation. Because of the reaction of the Counter-Reformation, Catholic theology insisted on the objective factors: that the object of the faith is presented by the Church as its norm (*ministra objecti*) and that it is possible to rationally prove the fact of revelation. In contrast with the patristic and medieval tradition which maintained that the light of faith makes us accept with certainty both the *fact* and the *contents* of revelation, Catholic theology began to yield to a very debatable distinction between the *contents* (the whole of unprovable truths) and the *fact* of revelation which, as such, could be proved. This tendency was encouraged by the controversies with the Rationalists and Deists of the Enlightenment who tried to reduce the truths of faith to truths that reason can comprehend.

At the very time that Catholic theology reacted against this dissolution of theology into philosophy by insisting on the obscure and unprovable character of strictly supernatural truths, it remained still imprisoned in this rationalism and tried to provide a rational proof of the fact of revelation at all costs. And so it developed a whole apologetic theology based on outward signs—the prophecies and especially the miracles—which were expected to provide the evidence for the fact that God revealed himself.

Apologetics as an Objective Science

And so in the 18th century we find manuals of apologetics which try to defend the truth of the Catholic religion against both the Rationalists and the Protestants by following a plan in three parts: (1) the existence of God and of religion (*demonstratio religiosa*); (2) the existence of the true religion (*demonstratio christiana*).[8] However, it is not until the beginning of the 20th century that we see the appearance of treatises in which the position of apologetics is explained with regard to both philosophy and dogmatic theology. In this field two works were outstanding: P. Gardeil's *La crédibilité et l'apologétique* (1908) and R. Garrigou-Lagrange's *De Revelatione* (1930).

The authors of these various projects had two things in common. First of all, they wanted to situate the science of apologetics within the faith, because apologetics cannot prove its own starting point, which is revelation, but only the credibility of this revelation. Second, because of their obsession with rationalism, they wanted at the same time to build up an objective science that could produce a maximum of evidence. According to Gardeil, "Apologetics is the science of the rational credibility of divine revelation." Its object is the credibility of Catholic dogma: "Credibility is the quality which Catholic dogma possesses because of the divine witness." For it is indeed "a property of revelation to be demonstrable by natural reason." By its formal object apologetics is therefore theological, while in its method it is a strictly rational and logical science. In the same way, Garrigou-Lagrange maintained that the proper function of apologetics is to present the revealed religion "in the light of the evidence for its credibility" (*sub ratione credibilitatis evidentiae*). It presupposes the faith but only appeals to rational arguments.[9]

The Failure of Apologetics as an Objective Science

During the last thirty years we have become far more aware of the grave limitations of the traditional apologetics of the textbooks, particularly with regard to its concept of *revelation*, and this mainly through the renewal that took place in biblical studies. One may say that the *Constitution on Divine Revelation* of Vatican Council II has confirmed the progress which has taken place in fundamental theology during the last thirty years.[10] This no longer starts, as in the past, with an *a priori* concept of general revelation but, deliberately following the historical and theological method, proceeds straightaway from the concrete event of the revelation accomplished in Jesus Christ.

One of the great weaknesses of apologetics as an objective science lay in thinking that credibility was a characteristic that extended equally to all dogmas without having theologically and critically examined the key dogma of revelation itself. Revelation is a *transcendental* theological category in the sense that it precedes every single theological datum, while at the same time containing it.[11] That is why any fundamental theology which wants to be a critical justification of the *foundations* of theology must begin with a study of the notion of revelation. This revelation is not something that can be proved by sheer rational argument. It is the basic presupposition from which we start, and without which any truth that theology deals with collapses. We can therefore not proceed, as the old treatises on apologetics did, by asking ourselves the question of the possibility, fittingness and need of revelation. We have to start straightaway with the event of revelation as recorded in Scripture and then try to disentangle its overall significance for the believer and for man in general in a given cultural situation.

Because of the *a priori* method used by the old apologetics, one can understand that the expression "apologetics" is being rejected more and more widely, and that the term "fundamental theology" is preferred as the science of the foundation of the faith (and hence of theology)—that is, the science of the dogma of revelation itself. "Thus setting up the apology of this dogma, and hence demonstrating its credibility, we will then *ipso facto* ensure the credibility of all other dogmas which spring from it; it will provide the faith with a foundation and theology with its principles."[12]

Another shortcoming of apologetics as an objective science, and the direct result of its abstract notion of revelation, is that it takes as obvious the distinction between "what God reveals" and the fact "that God reveals." This view leads to a dangerously extrinsic distinction between the judgment of credibility of the fact of revelation and the assent in faith to the contents of that revelation. It presupposes an intellectual notion of revelation as a "communication of truths that cannot be proved" and it forgets that it is the very fact of revelation which is the object of the Good News of the Gospel. Some authors might be tempted, under the influence of Bultmann, to say that the order is wrong, because one could say that all men can already have a certain preliminary understanding of the content of revelation as the message of salvation but that the unforeseeable and unprovable character of the Good News lies in the fact that this salvation is already in fact given to us in Jesus Christ.[13]

As long as the wholly abstract notion prevailed of a revelation conceived as communication of supernatural truths, it was possible to pretend that one could demonstrate the evidence of the credibility of the fact of revelation (i.e., such a revelation is neither physically nor morally contrary to God or man) without bothering about the content. When we return to the biblical— that is, the historical, personalist and christocentric—notion of revelation as put forth in the *Constitution on Divine Revelation*, we can see that the exact dividing line between fundamental and dogmatic theology is difficult to trace. Fundamental theology also takes into account matter belonging to other dogmatic treatises. But we still have to ask ourselves how fundamental theology specifically looks at the mysteries of faith.

Finally we must mention the most serious deficiency of apologetics as an objective science, and the major reason why it is criticized by modern apologists. The objection is that the old apologetics proceeded with a *rational credibility* which nowhere joined up with the *lived credibility of the believer*. Hence the deceptive character of those scientific manuals of apologetics which try to provide decisive arguments of a metaphysical, physical and historical nature to prove the truth of the Christian religion and the Catholic Church, and which have never convinced anyone yet. Today we are more aware of the mistake of using an apologetic method derived from the religious controversies of the past and collecting external motives of credibility to explain how and why a definite concrete person should accept the faith.

Here we see how strongly the method and favorite themes of any fundamental theology are influenced by the social and cultural context. One can only court failure by trying to apply today a method of apologetics which flourished in the cultural climate of the Enlightenment. As J. Walgrave put it: "For the modern man, deductive reason is no longer a 'separate mental faculty' (*intellectus separatus*) which defines the truth of life by its own light, in order to apply it afterward to practical conduct. It has become increasingly evident that thought at large—and thought about the truths of life particularly—cannot hover somewhere above or outside life, but that it can only move within conscious life itself, taken as a whole."[14]

In other words, when we are dealing with a value like religion, the judgment of credibility cannot be limited to mere reason. It depends on a free and existential option, or at least on some basic ethical judgment. At the present time, therefore, while the rational justification of the faith remains a valid pursuit, such a justification will no longer limit itself to extrinsic proofs for the divine origin of Christianity, but will rather start with an explanation of what it means to live the faith today within the Church and within this world. To vindicate the faith is a matter of showing the meaning of Christianity for the conscience of someone who is already involved morally in an historical situation.

The Human Credibility of Christianity

These grave defects of objective, too purely intellectual and too extrinsic apologetics explain the success of what has been called "the apologetics of immanence" (cf. Blondel's *L'Action*, 1893) and Rousselot's view.[15] The merit of the so-called *subjective* apologetics was that it showed up the formal credibility of the other type, based only on rational argument and ignoring such affective elements as the "intention of belief," regarding them as but a skeleton, a mere abstraction.

During the last thirty years, however, an attempt has been made to overcome the false dilemma between an objective and a subjective apologetics. Authors use the term *integral apologetics* to describe a kind of apologetics which tries to maintain the value of the affective factors that are implied in real credibility. This does not mean that it has become a theology of conversion or "the art" of apologetics, but rather that it tries to analyze the objective structures of the subjective faith. And here Blondel's analysis of the internal logic of human action has proved most fruitful. In this way, the object of such an apologetic approach is no longer merely the rational credibility, but the *human credibility* of Christianity.[16] And we have at last clearly realized that it is simply not enough to try to vindicate the truth of Christianity by starting from historical proofs.

In conclusion, then, one can understand why the term "fundamental theology" is now preferred to describe Christian apologetics. It is not simply that in an age of dialogue the word "apologetics" is discredited. It is rather, and more profoundly, that we have become conscious of the weakness of apologetics when it pretends to be able to prove the *fact* of revelation on historical grounds. We can only be sure of divine revelation within the experience of faith. From the start, fundamental theology insists on its theological and historical character. It proceeds to a *critical* examination of the twofold foundation of Christian existence—namely revelation and faith. And within this critical process it exercises its function of *justifying* the validity of both. It bases the rational character of the act of faith on the way Christianity corresponds to the existence of man in all its dimensions.[17] I would like for a moment to concentrate on this major preoccupation of fundamental theology by stressing its *anthropocentric* approach.

II
THE ANTHROPOCENTRIC APPROACH OF FUNDAMENTAL THEOLOGY

When we try to explain the development that has taken place in fundamental theology during the last thirty years, we realize that it fits in with the urge to overcome the intellectualist and objectivist way in which neo-Thomism saw the problems. We can no longer rest content with the analysis of a purely rational credibility because this no longer corresponds to our modern frame of mind. If fundamental theology aims at "justifying" the faith in the eyes of both the believer and the unbeliever, it has to take into account the philosophical and cultural situation which conditions our mind. Therefore, the best students of fundamental theology will take note of the changes that have affected human understanding since Kant; they will take man's historicity much more seriously, and they will not overlook the fact that today we have reached the age of criticism, or, rather, of hermeneutics. This is the background to that "anthropocentric" concern which is evident in so much work in fundamental theology today.

The Functional Orientation of Theology

One might define the program of fundamental theology by saying that it must deal with the *anthropocentric dimension of the whole of theology*. This consideration of the human viewpoint is something generally required for all dogmatic theology, but it is the specific function of fundamental theology to provide a critical vindication of dogmatic theology from the angle of a transcendental analysis of man.

Traditional theology, which found its highest expression in Thomas Aquinas, represents an admirable attempt to understand the eternal content of the mystery of God and the mysteries of faith. Modern theology is more concerned with bringing out the *meaning* of the Christian mystery as a whole for people today. It therefore wants to be more existential, more anthropocentric. This tendency, moreover, corresponds to the development of theological thought about revelation, of which I have already spoken. Biblical revelation only speaks to us of God as he is in himself insofar as it is implied in his action for *us*; it is always a dispensation and functional—that is, "saving." On the other hand, one cannot separate thinking about the fulfillment of revelation in history from thinking about its fulfillment in the believer. In contrast with the extrinsic explanations of revelation as a communication of supernatural truths addressed to the human subject as a passive receptacle, we must say that the meaningful activity of God's people becomes a constitutive element in revelation itself. We may therefore say that revelation is already a tradition and even hermeneutical.

Finally, modern theology attempts to draw the consequences of Bultmann's basic intuition about the necessary preunderstanding which is involved whenever we try to read again the Christian message. It wants to provide all at once and inseparably an interpretation of the Word of God and of man's existence. There is no revelation in the full sense if the gift of God's original Word does not coincide with a revelation of man to himself. As Paul Ricoeur put it: "Revelation as such is an opening up of existence, a possibility of existing."[18] The understanding of Christianity can therefore not be severed from reflection upon man as a mysterious opening up, a looking for meaning and direction.

A number of authors therefore seek to develop a dialectic of man's existence where Christianity can be seen as giving meaning and fulfillment to mankind. I have already alluded to H. Bouillard's plan for an apologetic which, following Blondel, starts from the will as passing from the phase of striving to that of full determination, and tries to show that the Christian faith is the necessary, though inaccessible, condition of man's destiny. But I would like to refer especially to Karl Rahner's ideas about the necessary relation between theology and transcendental anthropology.

*The Anthropocentric Approach
and the Transcendental Problem*

"Transcendental" here means the *a priori* condition for the life of the spirit, that which makes it possible for anything to become the object of thought, will or love. For Rahner, God is the *a priori* condition of all our spiritual activity. To adopt a transcendental reference (*problématique*) or to treat the whole of dogma as transcendental anthropology means "to investigate, in regard to any topic of dogma, the conditions of its knowledge in the subject—here, in the theologian; it will show that there are indeed *a priori* conditions for the knowledge of this topic, and that these conditions already imply something of this topic or object, and of the way, the method and the limits of its being known."[19]

To apply a transcendental method to theology means, finally, to show the link between dogmatic statements and human experience as the object of reflection. Revelation is always concerned with man's salvation. Now, only too often dogmatic statements of the Christian faith appear esoteric or mythical because they show no connection with man's experience in his effort to understand himself. It is therefore up to the theologian to bring out the anthropocentric dimension of the statements of faith—that is, to show the link between what these statements envisage and man's self-understanding. I would say that this is the special function of the fundamental theologian because, by laying bare this anthropocentric dimension of all theology, he shows at the same time that the mysteries of the Christian faith are credible.

Karl Rahner does not, of course, deny the radically "theocentric" character of Christian theology insofar as its content is concerned. But he thinks that if we take the anthropological orientation of modern philosophy seriously, we must try to show the meaning of revelation as intelligible for our contemporaries on the basis of a profoundly "anthropocentric" understanding.

Clearly, the danger of such an approach is that it might take the meaning out of the gratuitousness of revelation as the history of salvation and that "one might deduce by some strict and necessary logic all the theological propositions from this single experience of oneself as the source of their objectivity and their conceptual articulation."[20] Rahner explicitly rejects this new kind of modernism. But the whole problem of a fundamental theology which thus makes use of the transcendental method is the delicate articulation of the relation between man's existence as the transcendental *a priori* condition of the faith and Christianity as the *a posteriori* historical condition. In fact, Rahner can only avoid the danger of a necessary deduction by using an anthropology which already owes much to the light of revelation. His concept of theology as transcendental anthropology is unintelligible if one does not know his bold thesis about the relation between grace and nature. One can show a link between the structures of human existence and the content of dogmatic statements by pointing to the fact that " 'nature,' understood as spiritual, personal and transcendental, is an intrinsic, constitutive and necessary element, not of grace as such, seen in the abstract, but of the reality and the event in which grace can be effectively given."[21]

Therefore, one cannot reproach Rahner with starting from an anthropology which would owe nothing to revelation and which would reduce this revelation to its own measure,[22] but one could object that his idea of the autonomy of philosophy is debatable. However, here we get involved in the permanent controversy about the relation between philosophy of religion and fundamental theology. In any case, Blondel has proved that it is possible to respect the autonomy of philosophy without depriving oneself of the new philosophical contribution brought about by revelation.

Fundamental and Dogmatic Theology

At present it is more important to stress that this transcendental character of fundamental theology forces us to reassess the relation between fundamental theology and dogmatic theology. If many people today doubt the *fact* of divine revelation, the reason is that they have difficulties with the *content* of revelation. It would therefore seem that the critical and justifying function of fundamental theology must operate in every dogmatic treatise. As Rahner suggests, we should have a far greater interpenetration of fundamental theology and dogma than we have at present.[23] Without denying that the proper function of special dogmatic theology is to arrive at an understanding of the content of each mystery of faith, it would appear true to say that the more theology becomes a hermeneutical science, the more the distinction between fundamental theology and dogmatic theology will tend to get submerged.

Whereas Rahner speaks about the "anthropocentrism" of theology, one might just as well speak about its need to be hermeneutical, in the very broad sense that we cannot assert anything about God which does not imply some assertion about man. In other words, we need a theological knowledge concerned not only with knowing the objective truth of dogmatic statements but also with their meaning for man today. When we understand the hermeneutical function of theology, we are simply following up the implications of Heidegger's hermeneutical phenomenology when he says that all knowledge of being can only be arrived at in the light of that particular being which examines being—namely, man.[24]

We should be able to maintain this hermeneutical requirement without slipping into the extremes of an impenitent Bultmannism which runs the risk of reducing theology to mere anthropology. I can only interpret history through the living interpretation of myself as an historical being constantly tending toward self-fulfillment. As Schillebeeckx said: "Understanding the faith and self-interpretation cannot be separated."[25]

Today, therefore, we would define fundamental theology as the *critical* and *hermeneutical* function of all theology. It is "critical" in the sense that it analyzes the condition of historical possibility and the transcendental condition of the faith: on the one hand, the event of revelation, and, on the other, man's existence as the *a priori* condition of the faith. Its proper and complex function is to let the *a priori* condition and the historical *a posteriori* condition of the faith illuminate each other. It is "hermeneutical" in the sense that it tries to disentangle the lasting significance of the statements of faith in their scriptural, dogmatic and theological form through man's understanding of himself and of his relation to the world.

On the basis of what has been said, we might divide the course in fundamental theology into two major sections: the study of the fulfillment of revelation in history, and the fulfillment of revelation in the believing subject. But we should stress that this is a formal distinction, since revelation necessarily implies human subjectivity where it is fulfilled in faith, and one cannot study the faith without considering its relation to the historical event of revelation.

We see, then, that while it is true that this critical and hermeneutical function is required today for all theology, it finds a particularly explicit expression in the two major sections of any fundamental theology: revelation and faith.

III
Fundamental Theology Must Look to the Future

I have tried to bring out the anthropocentric orientation of modern fundamental theology. This orientation must be interpreted as a sign of the historical situation with which faith is presented in this world. Many people accept Christianity in general while feeling ill at ease with this or that particular statement of the Christian faith. It would be precisely the task of this new kind of fundamental theology, advocated by Rahner, to provide a "vindication of the faith, lived before it is thought."[26] We should put together what, at the existential prescientific level, would *justify* the belief of an educated man today (because faith must be "reasonable").[27]

Yet, it seems clear from the more recent and significant studies in this field that authors have already begun to see the limitations and dangers of this inflation of anthropology. There is a fear that we may make man the measure of the Word of God. It is also said against the use of the transcendental dimension that it puts transcendental subjectivity before man as an historical and political being, and that it therefore overcomes idealism only in appearance.

Man as the Measure of Revelation

One could level the same reproach at both the anthropological intent of fundamental theology and Bultmann's existential hermeneutics. Under the pretext that the language of revelation has become unintelligible for many people today, it has been so carefully adapted to their understanding that the very content of the message is in danger of losing all meaning. God has been reduced to the meaning he may have for man as he understands himself and his relation to others, and so man has become the measure of revelation.

In one of the most important contributions to today's fundamental theology, Hans Urs von Balthasar has sounded a serious warning against the dangers of anthropocentrism in theology. Without quoting Rahner directly, he sees in the use of the immanent or transcendental method the danger of "a hidden and sometimes explicit philosophizing where the internal measure of the seeking spirit—seen as empty, or simply vacant, or as the 'restless heart,' or as a *potentia obedientialis* (a natural tendency to seek God), etc.—is somehow turned into the measure of revelation."[28] He thinks that this kind of tendency finds its extreme expression in modernism "where the objective facts of revelation become totally dependent on the subjective internal and dynamic relationship of revelation between God and the soul, and are only valid for the Christian insofar as they effectively support and foster this dynamic relationship."[29]

In contrast with this, von Balthasar approaches the question from a contemplative angle, and tries to show the splendor of the figure of Christ (he calls it the aesthetic aspect of revelation) as the manifestation and celebration of absolute love—that is, the love which reigns within the Trinity and God's love for mankind: "Only love is worthy of belief." Christ is the concrete form of absolute love; he finds his vindication in himself, whatever the subjective condition of man: "The figure we meet in history is convincing in itself because the light in which it manifests itself radiates of its own strength and clearly proves itself in its own radiation."[30]

Basically, von Balthasar reminds the theologians that in-

stead of trying to explain the newness of revelation on the basis
of some previous condition which falls back ultimately on
human reason, they should let the revelation manifest its meaning on the basis of its concrete origin, the figure of the Word incarnate. One might be inclined to say that von Balthasar has
taken Heidegger's warning very seriously: "As long as the
building of anthropological and sociological as well as existentialist concepts has not been overcome and abandoned, theology
will never acquire the freedom to express what it has been entrusted with."[31]

This is not the place to join in the controversy about a
pluralistic theology within Christianity. Following Malevez, I
would simply point out that von Balthasar himself cannot wholly do without some kind of pre-understanding. I can only appre-
hend the beauty of the mystery of Christ if I already have
within me some kind of norm of beauty, and it is because I per-
ceive there a certain affinity that I can come to credibility.[32] It
is the function of the fundamental theologian to analyze and or-
ganize this pre-comprehension. On the other hand, even in Bultmann the historical *a posteriori* of the revelation as the event of
grace can never be deduced from the comprehension of man.
Revelation is defined precisely by the fact that it is beyond the
power of man. Finally, I repeat that we should not forget that
the transcendental anthropology from which theologians like
Rahner start to show the credibility of Christianity already
owes a great deal to the light of revelation.

An Excessively Individualistic Concept of Man

The transcendental approach is not only attacked by those
who maintain that it reduces the mystery content of revelation
too much to man's measure. Others object that it is too bound
up with individualistic categories and with faith in the *present*
phase as an existential encounter between God and man. A
purely transcendental, personalist and existential theology becomes inadequate as soon as in this age of "secularization" the
new understanding of the world requires a more penetrating

reflection on the relations between the Christian faith and the world. In particular, it is unable to treat the world as *history* with the seriousness it demands. The most lucid protagonists of this new tendency are the Protestant J. Moltmann and the Catholic J.B. Metz.[33] They would prefer to say that the main theme of fundamental theology is no longer the relation between theory and practice. They want it to concentrate on the social and political implications of the Christian faith. This is why fundamental theology will increasingly become the platform for the dialogue between faith and the human sciences, and not only between faith and philosophy as in the past.

Fundamental Theology as "Political Theology"

According to these authors, in the post-religious situation of our time, when the world is no longer an object of contemplation but an immense workshop and man is defined by his boundless capacity to build a world that is always new, it is the proper function of fundamental theology to spell out the "dimension of the future" and the social-political orientation of Christianity. It should particularly show the biblical foundation (the Old Testament is about the "promise") of this orientation toward the future which characterizes our modern culture and toward an understanding of the world as history which results from it.

In other words, it is the dimension of the *future* which enables our thought to reach beyond the limitations of an anthropocentric theology too exclusively concerned with the value of the decision of faith for the present moment. With this dimension of the future, one can interpret "the world as history, history as the history of the end, faith as hope and theology as eschatology."[34] For J.B. Metz it is not enough that fundamental theology introduces the anthropocentric dimension into the whole of theology; our present spiritual situation urgently requires that we lay bare the "eschatological dimension" of all theology: "Eschatology is not just one discipline side by side with other disciplines. It is the fundamental dimension which determines, and shapes, every theological development, particularly with regard to the world. The attempt to interpret the whole of theology on an existential or personalist basis is an important contribution to theology. . . . But this existential and 'anthropocentric' theology can easily remain foreign to the world and to history if eschatology is not brought in as an essential element. Only in the eschatological perspective of hope can the world appear as history. Only when we understand the world as history can our free action be given its rightful place: in the center."[35]

The world is nothing but an immense field of potentiality waiting for the free creativity of man striving toward the future with his whole being. In this age of secularization the only theology that can account for both the Christian hope and the hope of this earth simultaneously is neither a theology of the cosmos nor a transcendental theology of man's existence, but a *political theology*—i.e., a theology which takes the social and political dimension of man seriously, in the way man understands himself today. According to J.B. Metz, the function of such a theology is twofold. On the one hand, it will critically examine the individualistic tendency still current among contemporary theologians. No doubt, the private sector and the ineffable encounter between God and individual man constitute the specific territory of existential hermeneutics and a kind of theological personalism. On the other hand, "the positive function of political theology tries to determine a new kind of relationship between religion and society, between the Church and the social reality of public life, between an eschatological faith and the practical reality of society."[36]

Fundamental Theology and the Border Problems between Church and World

This new "political" trend in fundamental theology shows how much its problems are conditioned by the situation of the faith in this world. No doubt, the traditional themes of fundamental theology (the historical and rational foundations of

Christianity and the critical explanation of the essence, method and language of theology) require more penetrating research and will always do so. But if the primary task of fundamental theology is to justify Christian hope in a given historical situation, it is there that we must sort out the relations between the Church and the world on the lines of the *Pastoral Constitution on the Church in the Modern World*. The theologian must not only bear witness to the permanent aspects of the Word of God, but he must also deal with the new human issues in their relation to the content of revelation. He must begin by *sharing* in man's understanding of himself, his world and his future, so that he can judge the great issues which beset the Christian conscience with a genuine critical understanding in the light of the faith. As Schillebeeckx said: "To ask about the inspiration of the Gospel as detached from the concrete content of our own existential experience is to ask a question without substance, and to this one can only give an unrelated and existentially meaningless answer."[37] However, all too often both believers and nonbelievers have the impression that the Christian Churches continue to confess a doctrine that is admirable but irrelevant to man's most urgent problems. It is not good enough to claim an admirable nature for Christianity and then to ignore the failures of Christianity in history. The critical and liberating force of the Gospel must be manifested in thought and action. The answer of the Gospel will always be paradoxical. It disputes man's self-sufficiency, and it doubts excessively optimistic ideologies about man's future. But at the same time, precisely in virtue of its eschatological dimension, it sets man free and urges him on in his earthly expectations: the humanization of man, the socialization of mankind, and the building of an order of universal peace and justice.

I cannot list here all the border problems with which a modern fundamental theology should concern itself. But one may confidently assert that they will primarily concern the relations between faith and the new forms of atheism (the theology of unbelief), the Christian interpretation of ideological and religious pluralism (theology of non-Christian religions), the confrontation between faith and the political and social reality (theology of violence), and the reinterpretation of Christian life in the context of a secularized world (theology of the realities of this world).

In conclusion, it seems right to say that the most active research in fundamental theology is trying to reach beyond the objectivism of neo-Scholastic theology as well as the anthropocentrism of existential theology. We are witnessing the birth of a new kind of fundamental theology which intends to embody man's new self-understanding, particularly his understanding of the future on this earth. As in the past it tries to make Christianity credible, but by stressing its social and eschatological dimension. And only those who have forgotten the unique destiny of the Church and the world in God's plan will be astonished to see fundamental theology so ardently pursue extra-theological problems.

2. Dogmatic Theology in the Hermeneutic Age

In choosing this title I would like to see where present research in dogmatic theology is, while taking proper account of the fact that theology is tending to become less dogmatic and more hermeneutic.

We shall begin by reflecting on the current crisis in dogmatic theology and shall try to give a diagnosis. It is unquestionable that the theology we call speculative is experiencing an unprecedented crisis at its foundations. However, this situation brings along with it its own share of good fortune for the renewal of theology. I shall therefore attempt to single out what seem to me to be most characteristic and promising in the current trends in dogmatics. Then, in a third part, I shall be more explicit about some of the methodological consequences of this new orientation in dogmatics. And so the approach that will be followed will be to start from present factors that condition dogmatic theology in order to bring to light certain contents of contemporary theology and to open out onto problems of method. However, questions of method already will have been brought up in the first two parts.

In order to prevent any misunderstanding, it is wise to make clear the point that I shall speak of theological research over and above denominational divisions, since it is so true today that the cleavages among the various theological trends do not run along the boundaries of different Christian denominations.

I

THE CURRENT UNREST IN DOGMATIC THEOLOGY

One must have courage to face what can be called a certain disarray in dogmatic theology. It is going through an identity crisis.[1] There are still theology courses; there are still new publications in theology; we are still being invited to numerous meetings and seminars to give "the theologian's point of view." But sometimes it is not very clear from what standpoint theologians are speaking. We are also aware of the difficulties theology departments are encountering in building up a coherent program of dogmatic theology and in doing things in such a way that the teaching of dogmatics will keep its privileged and irreplaceable role in relation to what is now being taught in exegesis, history, philosophy, and the human sciences of religion.

Let us very quickly try to diagnose the causes of this situation.

The Phenomenon of Secularization

The phenomenon of secularization more radically affects dogmatic theology than the Church itself and the current forms of Christian service among men. What I mean is that the Christian Churches still make up an integral part of our Western society and that Christianity continues to play a considerable historical role, but often at the price of adaptation which is increasingly flexible to modern man's new ways of thinking and acting, and at the price of reducing the dogmatic content of the Christian faith to a human *ethos* which is general enough for Christians and non-Christians who believe in the future of man to be at ease with one another.

To the extent that the traditional formulations of the Christian faith remain the starting point and the norm for dogmatic theology, this kind of theology is now being relegated to the sidelines, even within the Church. It is becoming an "academic" theology confined to the ghetto of the theologians and theology departments. It no longer fulfills its essential function in the

Church: the service of the proclamation of the faith. Even if out of a need for safety, an "attending theologian," as it is called, is consulted, we are witnessing a rather disturbing break between catechesis or preaching and learned theology. Between scientific exegesis which is more and more sure of its methods and living preaching which out of necessity is attempting to formulate the content of the faith in a new way, dogmatic theology is assuming its mediating function rather poorly. This kind of situation will go on as long as theology is content to justify and explain the traditional statements of the faith instead of devoting itself to a creative revival of these same statements within the context of contemporary thought.

The Epistemological Uncertainty of Dogmatic Theology

As I said above: Theologians still have a lot to say, but they do not know from what standpoint they are speaking. The "crisis at the foundations" is not confined to theology. Philosophy is being subjected to the same trial. But, in virtue of its very nature and its somewhat undefined relationship to philosophy, it is understandable that theology would be even harder pressed to justify its epistemological choices. It has always been that way, but we are becoming more acutely aware of the breakup of the traditional theological realm which is understood as the scientific coherence of a certain number of sources. Theology in the Middle Ages legitimately occupied the first place in a coordinated body of knowledge and there was no gap between the language of theology and the cultural language of the times. Theology could claim to be the "regina scientiarum" as long as the sciences in the modern sense of the word had not yet been born.

Today, what do we see? The former realm of theology as a constituted science, hierarchically organized and in command of its language, is being fragmented between "exegesis" which has the legitimate claim to being scientific in the modern sense of the word, a polymorphous philosophical discourse which, depending on the treatise, borrows its themes from traditional ontology, German idealism, the different modern existentialisms, or a hermeneutics of scriptural and dogmatic language which has not yet settled on its methods and criteria.

In the face of this uncertainty, how can we be surprised if some theology students who have known the positivity and rigor of the modern sciences are cool toward dogmatic theology and are readily turning to the human sciences of religion which are imperceptibly gnawing away at the field of traditional theology.

Moreover, I do not think that theological language can be a *unitary* language: The material object of theology is too diversified and it is inevitable that various kinds of language will be used; those of the existential philosophies and those of the sciences of man. But precisely, if theology wants to have its autonomy respected in its dialogue with philosophy and the sciences of man, it must meet the condition of being able to justify its procedures, its methods, and its own proper criteria. To speak as certain linguists do, theological language is not only *performative* or involvement language; it is a *statement* language, a language which is based on the positivity of revelation and its historical signs. It must therefore have its own criteria of truth.

Today some people no longer want to call theology a *science*. But following the lead of the hermeneutic sciences it can legitimately aspire to a *scientific status* to the extent that it proceeds in methodical and critical fashion to an ordered knowledge of its object.[2] However, the built-in weakness of theological discourse in relation to the ideal of a perfect conceptual systematization is due to the very nature of its object, a God that is not a region of what exists, and to the fact that it speaks of man in his most general terms. But this weakness also accounts for the greatness of theology. I would even say that it justifies the irreplaceable position of theology within the university. Its role in effect is to maintain the *openness* of all the particular forms of knowledge.[3]

The Gulf Between "Saying" and "Doing"

I would like to pinpoint a third reason for the present uneasiness of dogmatic theology. As we ascertained at the theology congress in Brussels, we have today two types of theology. There is a kind of theology which would above all seek to be the expression of the experience of a particular Christian community.[4] Its preoccupation is to maintain a living connection between *doing* (community-oriented) and *saying* (theological) in order to avoid the meaninglessness of a purely verbal orthodoxy.[5] **1906973**

Those who hold for the other type argue more in favor of a theology which would be a general theory of the Christian faith, aiming toward a universal scope beyond individual experiences. The risk inherent in such a design is to end up with generalities which no longer interest anybody. This was quite apparent at the theology congress in Brussels where a wide agreement was reached at the price of a definite toning down of the initial theses.

In the face of this two-way tendency, I would say that it will become more and more necessary for the Church to accept *theological pluralism* as an inevitable fact. But we must be well aware that this pluralism in fact creates new demands relative to the teaching of dogmatic theology. This pluralism is due to the situation both of the Church and of our culture. The historical life of the Church has always been the source (*locus theologicus*) for theology. Moreover, any theology which was no longer a science of Christian experience would be very much like an ideology. So, the great problem of the contemporary Church is the progressive diversification of communities, their commitments and their cultural expressions within the respect for the unity of the confession of the faith. As much as we might refuse to dissociate a theological diversification from the community experience which supports it, the theology of the future will necessarily be a pluralistic theology. Now we realize that one of the major difficulties in traditional theological teaching comes from the fact that this theoretical knowledge is not connected with the Christian practice of the ecclesial group to which it is addressed. We can no longer be satisfied to let dogmatic theology be merely the transmission of a ready-made body of knowledge. It must also aim toward a well thought-out expression of first-hand experience.

Finally I would add that theology finds itself confronted with an insurmountable philosophical pluralism. This pluralism has always existed, but in the past, as Karl Rahner says, a man could raise the claim that one philosophy, namely his own, was *the* philosophy.[6] Presently, such a claim is impossible from the sole fact that no one man is capable of adequately embracing all the sources of human experience. It is enough to look at the immense field of human sciences, where it is impossible to synthesize the results. There is no longer a total system of culture in the older sense of the word. Because of this insurmountable plurality of present experiences of existence, there will exist various theologies for this or that fragmentary aspect of human existence. None of these theologies can, however, claim to constitute a coherent and complete synthesis of the faith. This creates a new situation for the Magisterium, which refrains from judging any new theological language without first seeking to understand its philosophical and cultural presuppositions. This is even more the case if the Magisterium practically identifies itself with one particular school of theology.

II

CHARACTERISTIC FEATURES OF CONTEMPORARY THEOLOGY

After this cursory survey of the new conditioning factors in dogmatic theology, I would like to try to characterize the present theological turning-point. This will provide the opportunity to allude to the content of theological research. At the risk of over-simplifying, I would say that theology is tending to become a *non-metaphysical* theology, *non-authoritarian* and *hermeneutic.*

A Non-Metaphysical Theology

A short while ago I argued for a theology which would not be cut off from experience. But theology cannot be satisfied with being, as is so often the case, the justification of the attitudes and the involvement of this or that particular group. It would be wrong, precisely at a time when theology is criticized for being the self-justification of the institutional Church, to have the same conception of theology serving the ends of particular groups within the Church. Theology is only true to itself if it speaks about God to the men of our secularized society.

Moreover, for numerous reasons which I cannot bring up here, language about God causes some difficulty. This is why we are witnessing more or less radical re-interpretation of the traditional talk about God. This is true of the various "death of God" theologies or theologies of secularization. I would only like to turn to the crisis in the philosophical foundations of traditional language about God.

We could sum up the uncomfortable situation of the Western theologian as follows: At a time when the God-object of traditional metaphysics is dead, how can we still speak of God without relinquishing speculative discourse and without falling into anthropocentrism?

The "death of God" movement is only the extreme form of the crisis of the objectivity of God in contemporary theology.[7] In spite of the relative success of neo-Thomism, it was inevitable that traditional theology would feel the repercussion of the revolution which has taken place in philosophy. It could be said that since Kant, religious language has lost its ontological roots: God is tending to become little more than the postulate of moral action. The two theologians who have most influenced modern theology, Karl Barth and Bultmann, are also each in his own way, heirs of the Kantian critique.

We could fairly well characterize the way in which the problem of God is posed in contemporary theology by saying that there is an attempt to go beyond both *theological objectivism* and *theological existentialism*. The first, because it leads to false objectifications of God in metaphysical thought; the second, because it runs the risk of reducing the mystery of God to its meaning for man. Dogmatic theology is therefore seeking to get beyond these two dangers by a greater fidelity to revelation itself where the *en-soi* of God can be reached only in and through its "for us" ("pour nous") and by a greater care to avoid separating the talk about God from talk about man. Modern theology aspires to be a theology of the history of salvation and it also possesses the ambition to be a *theology of reality* which could overcome the metaphysical duality of God and the world. This "Christological concentration" of modern theology must be understood in this perspective.[8]

It seems to me that modern dogmatics should pose and resolve with renewed effort the ever present question of any Christian theology: the relations between theology and economics.

We could dispute the historical interpretation of the fate of Western metaphysics given by Heidegger. But in the light of what he has said about the hidden essence of metaphysics as "onto-theology," we are led to seriously question the lumping together of the "metaphysical" with the "theological" in Christian theology. Today we are more aware of the attempt of metaphysical theology to explain the God of revelation from the concept of God as absolute foundation of existence (cf. *infra*, pp. 54ff.). Is it not true that this attempt at explanation wound up in modern thought in the "death" of God as represented object, as concept?

In a courageous article by Gérard Granel you can read the following provocative lines despite a somewhat obscure style: "Therefore it is only today when the philosophical *theion* is beginning to be located, understood and deconstructible, that it is becoming possible to get into the work of its 'destruction' by a somewhat cartographical focusing in on its most important texts distinguishing the lines of *superimposition* where there are found, intermingled, the 'theological' coming properly from God and properly concerning God and the 'theological' from nature and on a purely ontological level where the metaphysical *treatment* of the *untreatable* difference is reflected."[9]

The demand of contemporary theology, when it endeavors to be more existential and personalistic, must be understood as a reaction against the objectivism of metaphysical theology which "explains" and "reduces" the newness of the revelation event. Bultmann especially has shown how much knowledge of God eludes the "subject-object" schema of metaphysical thought. According to him, speaking "about God" has no meaning since, at the very moment in which this language is applied, it has lost its object.

However, within Catholicism as well as Protestantism we are even more clearly perceiving the limits of *existential hermeneutics* in which God is reduced to the event of an encounter which changes "me," like certain Catholic essays in transcendental theology which place too much emphasis on the conditions for appropriating the reality of God by the subject and run the risk of reducing the mystery of God to the meaning it has for man. These theologians (Rahner and his followers) could be designated as theologians of *mediation*, in contrast to theologians like Barth and Urs von Balthasar who insist on the *positive character* of revelation.[10]

In any case, at a time when the God of metaphysics is being attacked, the task of dogmatic theology is to overcome the objectivism of traditional theology without falling into the anthropocentrism of the existential theologies. The crisis in metaphysical language could at least have the advantage of making us more attentive to what is entrusted to us in revelation and lead us to a re-reading of theological and dogmatic tradition by seeking to unveil what has often been obscured through the interpenetration of the metaphysical and Christian elements.

A theologian like Pannenberg proposes a quite new method in dogmatics when he affirms that the very word God can only be understood from the particularity of the history of Jesus and proposes a Christology which starts from the bottom up the message and history of Jesus, and not from the top down—the Word and its incarnation in the flesh.[11] When Dom Ghislain Lafont gives as the title on an excellent work on Christology the question: "Can we know God in Jesus Christ?" he already presupposes a prior notion of God. Is not the true question: "Who is the God that we know in Jesus Christ?"[12]

A Non-Authoritarian Theology

Under this somewhat puzzling title I would like in fact to point to one of the most promising orientations of contemporary theology, particularly regarding its dialogue with the human sciences of religion.

Especially since the Enlightenment, theology has no longer been entitled to inclusion among the academic disciplines because of its "authoritarian" character which is contradictory to the scientific ideal. And, even today, eminent academic specialists, who are often themselves former theologians, condescendingly characterize theology as a "self-interpretation" serving the ends of the ecclesial system. With this they contrast the "hetero-interpretation" of the human sciences of religion as the only rigorous interpretation.

To this we could reply that Catholic theology has long ceased to be merely the justification of the pronouncements of the Magisterium, and that the "authoritarian" character of theology does not come from any human authority, even the highest ecclesiastical jurisdiction, but from the authority of the Word of God itself.

However, we must go even further: It is the very authority of the Word of God itself, the fundamental nature of revelation, which contemporary theology is re-examining. All of this is intended to insure the credibility of Christianity which in the face of human reason can no longer accept the truth in the name of an authority.

In order to understand the import of what I am saying here, you should reflect on the significance of the transition from the *theologies of the word* to the *theology of history* within contemporary theology.[13] I shall limit myself to several summary remarks in line with my purpose.

It is a fact that Christian theology in the second half of the twentieth century aspires to be a theology of history which would overcome the distinction between the history of salvation and secular history. This is true of the various theologies of secularization, and especially true of authors like Pannenberg and Moltmann who want to go beyond the theologies of the word of Barth and Bultmann. It is also true of the Catholic essays in *political theology*, like those of Metz which seek to go beyond Rahner's transcendental problematics.

Within Protestantism there is an attempt to go beyond the anti-liberal problematics of the theologies of the word of Barth and Bultmann. The starting point common to both Barth and

Bultmann is the belief that historico-critical research as scientific observation of the event leaves no more room for the salvation event. Barth hypostasizes the Word of God and Bultmann demythologizes the kerygma in order to preserve its strength to call forth a response. Today there is an attempt to recapture the historical event beyond the kerygma and we are no longer so obsessed by the opposition between *Historie* and *Geschichte* as though historical research were fatal for the future of the faith.

A theology of history like Pannenberg's seeks to overcome the divorce between the faith and modern reason's rule of autonomy and thereby insure the credibility of Christianity. The faith is founded on something historical and therefore the domain of theology is not only that of the inaccessible and the unverifiable domain of the supernatural. Theology can then enter into dialogue with the other disciplines of the mind, particularly history.

What bothers Pannenberg about the theologies of the word is not so much the fact that they are existential theologies, but that they are "authoritarian" theologies, which is to say based on a "supernatural authority" outside of observable history.[14] It is then necessary to "depositivize," which means to overcome the Kantian separation between fact and meaning, between history and interpretation which in theology has resulted in both historicism and supernaturalism and which maintains even today ruinous opposition between historical exegesis and theological hermeneutics and between positive theology and speculative theology.

This rejection of an "authoritarian" theology is consistent with the nature of biblical hermeneutics which shows us that Scripture is more a testimony which only delivers its meaning when grasped in the movement of an historical tradition than a *given fact* directly inspired by God. This is also consistent with the modern rule of reason which will not agree to submit itself to a truth in the name of an authority—even that of God. Moreover, the proper sense of Christian revelation is not only a supernatural affirmation guaranteed by God, but an indirect revelation of God in and through history.

It is the historical otherness of the founding events of

Christianity which insures the objectivity of the faith and shelters it from the illusions of religious consciousness. Then we have a theology which will strive to take into account our cultural horizon, which includes atheism.

I have allowed myself to insist on this new orientation of theology inasmuch as it represents a healthy reaction against certain theologies of the word which in modern times have consecrated the incompatibility between faith and reason and have insisted in the very name of the Gospel on the divorce between the Word of God and the objectivity of the world. Theology may be defined as the self-interpretation of Christianity. But this interpretation is not just a pure repetition of the past and has other guarantees than faith alone as a supernatural gift. Theology bases itself on an historical objectivity. In this time of development in the human sciences of religion, theology should take the fullest account of the atheistic interpretations of Christianity; this would oblige it to carry out a beneficial self-criticism. But, on the other hand, theology should be capable of demonstrating that its own believing interpretation is also humanly and rationally legitimate. If we are faithful to our interpretation, it is not simply because of our obedience to the supernatural authority of the Word of God, but because we think it is the only one that can account for the objective fact of history.

In concluding this section I would not like to give the impression that the time for the theologies of the word is over, and that they must be replaced by the theology of history from now on. I am seeking only to point out significant trends. It is obvious that we must reject any overly radical opposition between *theology of the word* and *theology of history*. On one hand, the theologies of the word are not necessarily based on a hermeneutics built on the single notion of "word event" which is understood in an existential and psychologizing fashion. On the other hand, the theology of history cannot escape the demands of the hermeneutic problem which is the dialectic of event and meaning.

Moreover, I would somewhat criticize Pannenberg for treating theology too much like a hermeneutical problem. According to Moltmann's criticism, his conception of revelation is still under the sign of the Logos: it does not have enough of the character of a promise.[15] The theology of history should be more than a science of interpretation; it is a science of hope.

A Hermeneutical Theology

These several reflections on the non-authoritarian character of theology quite naturally lead us to see how theology is becoming less dogmatic and more hermeneutical.

When we read contemporary theological literature, we notice that its method no longer consists, as was the case in the recent past, in explaining and justifying the dogmatic teaching of the Church by showing its agreement with Scripture and tradition. It is much more a question of bringing out the permanent significance of the Word of God in its scriptural, dogmatic and theological forms, starting with the historical understanding that man has of himself and his cultural world. This work of decoding meaning is certainly a hermeneutical task par excellence.

But what do we mean when we speak of theology as being hermeneutical? Is this only a concession to the tastes of the day? I do not think it is enough to reiterate that hermeneutics as the science of the interpretation of biblical texts has always existed in Christian lands. We use an old term for designating a new concept when we characterize the *intellectus fidei* as a hermeneutical act. It is a question of bringing out the present meaning of a past text rather than deciding on the intelligibility of a true proposition.

I cannot deal here with the extremely complex question of the relations between the history of modern philosophy and the new manner in which the hermeneutical problem is being posed in Christianity. You may refer to Ricoeur's enlightening preface to the French translation of Bultmann's *Jesus.*[16]

There is obviously a close connection between wnat I was saying before about the crisis in metaphysical language and the desire to understand theology as hermeneutics. It is certain that once we accept the Kantian critique of knowledge, it becomes difficult to consider the object of theology as the knowledge of God and the object of revelation as a "body of doctrinal truths communicated by God." Its object in the strict sense of the word is a *text*, that of the Bible and its successive interpretations in tradition—a text to be known and therefore to be interpreted.

I do not know if the theologians who are so enthusiastic about hermeneutics always reckon with the undermining character of modern hermeneutics in regard to the proper logic of traditional theology. Greek logic was not unaware of the problem of interpretation. Aristotle even wrote *Peri Hermeneias*, but this was only an introduction to the analysis of propositions and his whole effort was to put aside shifts in meaning and equivocation. Greek logic rests on the univocity of statements.

Modern hermeneutics, on the other hand, underscores the plurality and the divergence of meanings, the historical succession of interpretations and the difficulty which exists in surmounting the conflict among interpretations. Everyone reads a text with his own prior understanding, from his own cultural background. When we are dealing with a biblical text, the problem of its truth is therefore going to be posed in another way. Can I still believe? As Ricoeur says, "something has been lost, irreparably lost, the immediacy of belief" (*Philosophie de la volonté*, vol. II, p. 326). We can no longer adhere to something without critically examining it. We cannot get out of the hermeneutical circle, the dialectic of believing and understanding. We begin by critically examining the text from the context in which it originated. And if it is true that in the end it is necessary to believe in order to understand, our faith will not be any the less a post-critical faith accepted in deepened simplicity.

But we need not only appeal to our philosophical modernity to understand the hermeneutical demand of contemporary theology. In Christian tradition the hermeneutical role of the New Testament in relation to the Old Testament has always been understood; likewise its interpreting role in relation to all of human existence. Today, however, we even more clearly understand that the message of the New Testament is itself a legacy, a letter, a text to be interpreted. In other words, the hermeneutical exigency comes from a double distance in time which needs to be bridged, not only the distance between the past event of revelation and the present of our own culture, but also the distance between the scriptural accounts and the historical events they report.

We can then understand how theological hermeneutics is not just a concession to fashion. It is consistent with the very nature of the Word of God and the Christian faith. Because the Word of God revealed in Jesus Christ is neither identical to the letter of Scripture nor to the letter of dogmatic pronouncements, it is impossible today to separate the problem of the reformulation of the language of the faith from its reinterpretation. Even on the level of Scripture we cannot avoid posing the problem of the "Word of God-human word" relation. I mean that the letter of Scripture as the writing down of a witness account is already interpretation. The believing experience of Israel or of the first Christian community enters in as a constitutive element with revelation itself.

Moreover, it is the very nature of the faith as holding on to the truth of the Christian message which establishes the necessity of a theological hermeneutics. Indeed, the truth of the Christian message is not separable from the historicity of our present relation to primitive Christianity. Today we more clearly understand that "understanding of the Faith" and "self-interpretation" are inseparable. I can only interpret the history of salvation in relation to the living interpretation that I give of myself as an historical being situated in a particular tradition and culture. Hermeneutics is the very demand of the faith, inasmuch as revealed truth is not a dead truth, but a living truth which is always transmitted in an historical medium and which needs to be constantly made present.

We can then define dogmatic theology as the actualization of the meaning of revelation for today. By that I am referring to a complex hermeneutical task which goes from Scripture of the first actualization of the Word of God up to its ultimate actualization in preaching, having gone through successive actualizations in tradition. We have been able to speak of a "hermeneutical arch" to designate this complex operation. Like any historical knowledge, the hermeneutical understanding will always be in reference to the historical origin of the affirmation of faith which determines its immediate meaning. The texts refer back to real events, and it is this historical objectivity that excludes any indefinite hermeneutical liberty. But the grasp of these texts will also have to be in reference to our contemporary situation and our questions about salvation. These two polarities are inseparable and only by joining them together can we come to a living comprehension.

The delicate task of the hermeneutical theologian is to avoid both falsifying the past and transmitting only a dead past under pretext of fidelity. The question can seriously be asked, given the present situation of the Church, whether we must prefer a verbal orthodoxy identical for everybody to a real appropriation of the same truth in different formulations. Theology should be faithful to an historical witness which is not at its disposal and at the same time contemporary in the strongest sense of the word. Th only way to respond to this double demand is to bring together a hermeneutics of the Word of God and a hermeneutics of human existence in all its dimensions.

III

The Hermeneutical Dimension of Theology and Its Methodological Consequences for Dogmatic Theology

Let me point out some of the changes that may be brought about by taking the hermeneutical function of theology seriously.[17]

Dogma and Scripture

One of the most urgent tasks of hermeneutical theology is to devote itself to a re-interpretation of the formulations of the faith in such a way that they will really "impinge" on the believing understanding of today. Theological reflection can no longer take as its starting point the formulations of the faith as though they had value in themselves independent of the meaning they contain.

This is not falling into relativism if we say that the dogmatic formulas themselves are inadequate human expressions within a determined cultural and religious context. The method of Catholic theology mainly consisted in reading Scripture in the light of the dogmas, but it neglected to carry out the reverse operation, which is re-interpreting the dogmatic formulas in the light of Scripture and the progress in exegesis.

In fact, as soon as we avoid identifying Scripture and the Word, we can understand the complementary role of dogma and Scripture as the Church progressively makes the revealed truth its own. Dogma helps in the interpretation of Scripture, since we read Scripture within the tradition of the Church. But Scripture itself helps in the interpretation of dogma. Scripture helps us to discern what is really confessed in a given historical formulation of the Word of God, which may no longer be fulfilling its role of actualizing the Word of God. As Walter Kasper says: "Scripture and Dogma are both witnesses to the Gospel, but they never express the Gospel in its entirety which remains an unwritten future."[18]

Positive Theology and Speculative Theology

The hermeneutical function of theology obliges us to rethink the always touchy relations between positive theology and speculative theology.

Traditionally, this distinction between positive and speculative theology rests on the overly convenient distinction between a *given* whose meaning could be known by placing our present understanding in brackets and then a speculative *construct* which would only have a remote relation to the given. This gave rise to a certain type of theology which started with a static analysis of the *given*, from which one could speculate for theoretical deductions and practical applications. Today, a hermeneutical reflection helps us to understand that there is no *auditus fidei* without *intellectus fidei.*

The distinction between positive theology and speculative theology has in modern times actually consecrated a certain divorce between reason and history in the method of theology.[19] Positive theology confined itself to the scrupulous stating of the *fides credenda* and did not escape a certain positivism. Speculative theology no longer took its roots in history.

We all agree upon questioning the threefold division in the method of dogmatic theology which came out of the counter-reformation—explanation of the doctrine of the Church, demonstration or explanation by Scripture and tradition, speculative deepening. But to do that, we would have to overcome the opposition between historical method and speculative method. And that is only possible if we apply another conception of theological *reason.* Further along I shall come back to what distinguishes historical reason and speculative reason (cf., *infra*, p. 75). I simply point out here that a dogmatist like Pannenberg, whose speculative boldness nobody could call into doubt, does not hesitate to use the historical method in theology.

Biblical Theology and Dogmatic Theology

Inasmuch as there is no exegesis which is not already hermeneutics, and as theology is tending to become a hermeneutics of the Word of God, we can wonder if the distinction between biblical and dogmatic theology still has meaning.

In any case I think that in the hermeneutical arch which goes from exegesis to preaching, dogmatic theology retains an indispensable role. Dogmatic theology and biblical theology are two inseparable and complementary tasks of theological endeavor in the Church.

First of all, the scope of dogmatic theology is wider than the immediate object of biblical theology, namely the body of canonical books. The dogmatist also integrates into his understanding of the Word of God the later interpretations of tradition and the Magisterium. In this way there is an ecclesial theology of the New Testament which is more than a biblical theology of the New Testament.

In the second place, because of the difference between the Bible as a book and the Word of God as an always present event, biblical theology cannot exhaust the function of theology, as the actualization of the meaning of the Word of God. Even if the biblical theologian has the ambition of making the Word of God present for today, his first and irreplaceable task is to restore for us the primitive meaning of the text. This implies interpreting the meaning of the events reported for the participants in and the witnesses to these events. This is why this first appropriation of the Word of God is not only the source or the starting point for theology, but its inviolable norm.

Dogmatic theology, then, attempts to actualize the permanent meaning of the Word of God in relation to man's new question with the aid of the new conceptual instruments at the disposal of human thought. The dogmatist will not be satisfied with reproducing the various interpretations of biblical theology by trying to harmonize them. He is rather going to understand them in another way, which is to say that he is going to make an "unsaid" ("non-dit") emerge from revelation while taking account of a double polarity—the global becoming of the faith of the Church and modern man's power of comprehension.

I should like to speak then of the complementary role of biblical hermeneutics and theological hermeneutics. What is expected of biblical hermeneutics is the guarantee of historical origin; it is a question of transmitting a message which is no longer being formulated. What is expected of theological hermeneutics, on the other hand, is the guarantee of communicability: It is a matter of making the Word of God the norm of interpretation for today.

Conclusion

At the conclusion of this quick over-view, it seems that we could reasonably speak of a renewal of dogmatic theology, while being aware that the task is immense and that it has only just begun. The future of theology depends on new vocations to theology, not only among the clergy but among the laity as well.

Unfortunately, the theologian today does not enjoy any great prestige in the world or even in the Church. Academic people judge theology as too "dogmatizing." In the eyes of many of the clergy, it appears as useless if not repressive and leaves a lot of the simple faithful cold.

I would, however, like to recall in concluding that the profession of theologian is by no means an archaic function in modern society. The theologian is certainly not a man from a ghetto; he is a man among men, both believers and non-believers. His mission does not only consist in justifying the decisions of the hierarchical Church. Nor any more is it confined to justifying the stand of this or that pressure group within the Church. And, in this regard, it is certain that contemporary theology does not always escape the dangers of pragmatism or ideological opportunism. It is rather in a rigorous confrontation with the various expressions of modern thought that theology will take on both its prophetic function and its scientific function.

The theologian above all should be among men the witness of a very ancient question which is nonetheless always being reborn—the question of God.

3. Non-Metaphysical Theology

Pascal's attack on the God of the philosophers is more relevant than ever. This is not simply because of an irreducible character attached to the experience of the living God of faith; theological language about God is being subjected to a radical critique as part of a general crisis of metaphysical language and arguments. The theologians themselves eagerly echo such phrases as "the end of metaphysics," "the death of the God of metaphysics," "the end of theism" and "the beginning of a post-metaphysical age." Some, far from taking fright at this collapse of traditional metaphysics, greet it as a liberating event for Christian theology. The suspect alliance between the God of the philosophers and the God of Jesus Christ is at last broken, and the theologian is finally free to say what he has been entrusted with by revelation. In this view the term "non-metaphysical theology" emphasizes one of the most promising characteristics of the theology of the future.

All this is part of a fundamental debate which includes in the first place an historical dimension concerned with the relations between the God of philosophy and the God of Christian theology in the history of Western thought. It includes, however, a philosophical dimension concerned with the nature of theological language in its relation to the actual experience of the believer. It is impossible to consider all the elements of this debate in this article; I want merely to remove some ambiguities in facile talk about "non-metaphysical theology." The expression has a legitimate sense if it is used to denounce the false objectifications of metaphysical theology or the privileged connection of theology with any particular metaphysics, but it is an empty phrase if it is used to mean that we can give up the ontological reference of theological language as a language about God.

I shall begin by looking at the critique of metaphysical language formulated by the representatives of radical, or "death-of-God," theology. I shall then ask what should be our attitude to the critique of *onto-theology*, as the hidden essence of traditional metaphysical theology. This will lead to a consideration of the attack on the objectivity of God by a certain theological existentialism. I then examine the new paths open to a non-metaphysical theology.

I

The Crisis of Language about God

In different ways, every death-of-God theologian is under the influence of the analytic philosophy of the Vienna Circle or of the Oxford school of "linguistic analysis," and asserts that metaphysical propositions are strictly speaking meaningless. We may quote the following characteristic lines of Wittgenstein's: "Most of the propositions and questions to be found in philosophical works are not false but nonsensical. . . . Most of the propositions and questions of philosophers arise from our failure to understand the logic of our language."[1]

But, for my present purpose, it is above all important to note that in the whole current of radical theology the old debate about the relation between the God of metaphysics and the God of faith has been completely overtaken. It is the very word "God" which lacks meaning. Van Buren, for example, can write: "Today we can no longer even understand Nietzsche's cry 'God is dead'. . . . The problem is that, for us, the word 'God' is dead." The question is therefore not about the possibility of metaphysical language about God. It is the much more radical question about the very possibility of language about God, whether this language is metaphysical or religious. Culturally, the death of metaphysics simply preceded the death of God in the history of Western thought, and the theologians of the death of God consider these two cultural events as identical symptoms of the "radically secular nature" of our culture.

One of the signs of this radical attitude is that for contemporary analytical philosophers the problem is no longer one of the *validity* of metaphysical or theological statements but one of their meaning.[2] For the atheist and even for the agnostic, the question of God still has a meaning, but for the neo-positivist analytical philosophy the very word "God" lacks meaning. Indeed, if the "verification principle" provides a criterion for distinguishing meaningful propositions, any proposition in which God occurs as subject is not even false but meaningless. It is very apt to talk of a "semantic atheism" distinct from classical forms of atheism.[3]

We thus have to understand the "death-of-God" theology as a desperate attempt to maintain a Christian theological language when the impossibility of a meaningful language about God has been accepted as an inescapable cultural fact. In the face of such a theology, the real debate is not about the legitimacy of a non-metaphysical theology but about whether it is possible at all to have a Christian theology which no longer mentions God. In our view a Christian theology *without* God is nonsense, or at least it is no more than a form of anthropology. It is possible to show that it is contradictory to continue to appeal to the lordship of Christ over the world and man, and at the same time to assert the total self-sufficiency of secular man and his inability to state the problem of God.

In fact, the most recent representatives of analytical philosophy, in particular those who take their inspiration from the later Wittgenstein, show an increasing interest in the study of religious language. They reject quite specifically the narrowness of the "verification principle" and believe that there are affirmations about reality which are totally meaningful even though they cannot be empirically verified. This is true, for example, in the moral and religious orders. In so far as it is an element of human behaviour, language shares its complexity. There are different "language games" which cannot be reduced to a single form. The "language game" to which the word "God" belongs is religion. We must certainly reformulate our language about God to take account of the limits of secular man's understanding, but if we can no longer talk about God then we cannot talk about the rest of religion.

If we admit that there can be meaningful accounts of reality which cannot be empirically verified, why deny that religious language in general and language about God in particular can be meaningful? To refuse to reduce the language to empirical accounts is to admit the possibility of *metaphysical* language. From the philosopher's point of view, theological language is necessarily metaphysical, at least in the very general sense that it is not empirically verifiable. The phrase "non-metaphysical theology" can mean a theology which does not use metaphysical categories and is not tied to a particular system of metaphysics. But, having regard to a criteriology of languages, theological language belongs to the category of metaphysical, or at least speculative, language in the sense that it is *transgressive* with regard to the immediate data of experience and bears, in principle, on a reality which is accessible only through an interpretation.[4]

II
The Critique of Onto-Theology

The "death-of-God" movement in theology is merely the most radical expression of the fundamental crisis facing contemporary theology. But in order to understand and assess the attempt to create a non-metaphysical Christian theology we must take account of Heidegger's critique of onto-theology, which is seen as the hidden essence of Western metaphysics. It is obviously possible to dispute the interpretation of the historical destiny of Western metaphysics put forward by Heidegger, but it would be impossible to spend too much time in considering the fact that for the first time in the history of Christian thought in the West we are in a philosophical situation which allows us seriously to question the association of the "metaphysical" and the "theological" in Christian theology.

According to Heidegger, the cultural death of God conceived of as an object is written into the very destiny of metaphysics from its origin. In fact it is the same movement in metaphysics which makes God the absolute foundation of existence and kills him. Right from the start metaphysics has been unable to ask questions about the totality of existence without immediately postulating a supreme existence as the basis of being. This desire to find a foundation deeper than given existence shows rational man's desire for representation. The hidden essence of traditional metaphysics is onto-theology, that is to say, the explanation of an existence by its being and of being by a supreme existence: "An existence is understood in terms of its reasons for being, in order that, being understood, it may come into man's power."[5] Greek metaphysics did not become "onto-theology" because it was absorbed into Christian theology; it was onto-theology from the start.

In the modern era, absolute Spirit and, finally, man have replaced God understood as the supreme Existence. In Hegel the spirit of man tends to become the spirit of God, and in Nietzsche we reach the murder of God by the self-foundation of the will to power. This reversal was possible because right from the beginning God was thought of as existence which man could control by representing. The fact of man's replacing God as the foundation is written into the movement of metaphysics itself in the form of the desire to explain the totality of the real by transcending it from a foundation.

This identification of the aim of Western metaphysics as a desire to explain, under the sign of the logos, invites us to undertake a critical re-reading of traditional theology as metaphysical theology. The history of Christian theology is in fact inseparable from the history of conceptions of being. And today the crisis of metaphysics in Heidegger's sense begins a new era for Christian theology, in which it is no longer possible to confuse the elements of theology deriving strictly from God, and those deriving from nature on a purely ontological level. In other words, theology is invited to be itself and to say what it has been given to say by revelation.[6] This is all the easier today, since the valuable work of biblical research is helping us to understand more and more clearly the specific originality of the Judaeo-Christian God.

The theology of Thomas Aquinas remains an unparalleled

achievement of Christian theology in the form of metaphysical theology. In interpreting the God who revealed himself to Moses in terms of being, Aquinas bridged the gulf between faith and knowledge and showed that the biblical God was identical with the God reached by the rational approach of the philosophers. Moreover, Aquinas' approach is thoroughly theological; he did not begin by working out an idea of God which he later identified with the God of revelation.[7] Nevertheless, by making the supreme Being the intelligible principle which made it possible to take account of all the attributes and works of God, Aquinas took a decision which was to have serious consequences for the future of Christian thought. In our effort to take seriously the relation of God to the history of salvation, we are even more aware today of the risks inherent in such a theological attempt. It may even be asked whether an ontological theology of this sort does not bear in itself in germ the danger of the false objectification of God which is the triumph of natural reason. In other words, does such a theology escape the destiny of Western metaphysics as Heidegger understands it? It seems hard to deny that Aquinas' science of theology is part of the onto-theological enterprise of metaphysics. In the first place it derives the truth of existences from the primary truth of their principle, absolute Being, and it also tries to make sense of, to explain, revealed mysteries on the basis of God understood as the cause and foundation of all that exists. The *Ipsum Esse subsistens* becomes the hermeneutic principle of all theology.

Even in the case of God's being, being is still thought of as the being of an existence. God is the first existence, *primum Ens*. This is very definitely representational thought in Heidegger's sense, thought which stands over against what it thinks and makes it present to itself. If this metaphysical thought is the inevitable destiny of being, we can even say (with Welte) that Aquinas' metaphysics "developed what was for its time the highest form of metaphysics, the influence of which was to extend for a long time, perhaps even throughout the time of the domination of metaphysics."[8] And if there was in fact in Aquinas "the seed of the possibility of going beyond metaphysics," that is, a very clear realization of how much of the divine

Ipsum Esse lay beyond conceptualization, this remained in the background: the later development of Thomist thought was affected by the increasing tendency to conceptualization.

The task of Christian theology at the end of metaphysics is therefore to make clear the hidden essence of the enterprise of metaphysical theology, its desire to explain revelation by starting from God conceived as the absolute foundation of existence. In metaphysical theology there is a rigorous reduction of the biblical attributes of God, particularly when they are expressed in verbal form, to the pure actuality of Being. This leads to inescapable difficulties if we really want to take seriously the "historical" actions of God (the creation, incarnation and divinization). The limitation of a metaphysical theology based solely on the analogy of being, with its strict distinction between proper and metaphorical divine names, is that it ignores the intelligibility proper to the great biblical symbols. The identity of God with absolute Being then becomes the ultimate criterion for the validity of language about God. This involves the risk of keeping only those elements of biblical language about God which can be formulated in the conceptual system of scientific theology. Aquinas, for example, tries to understand the history of salvation by starting from the necessary properties of God understood as absolute Being, but he does not show enough of the new understanding of the transcendence of God as love which is made available to us by the history of salvation. So in metaphysical theology, the triumph of explanatory thought, everything happens as if the deepest mystery of the God who reveals himself were "reduced" to a pre-existing foundation, derived ultimately from the logos of human reason. The legitimate ambition of a non-metaphysical theology would be to accept "reduction to mystery," that is, to think about the mystery of God only within the coming of truth which is revelation.

III

The Attack on the Objectivity of God

The realization of the hidden essence of metaphysical theology is inseparable from the critique of the objectivity of God in contemporary theology. Particularly within Protestant theology, there has been for half a century a radical critique of objective knowledge of God.[9] This radical critique is in continuity with Luther's protest against scholastic theology, but Barth and Bultmann are, each in his own way, heirs of the Kantian critique. They both want to go beyond the objectivism of metaphysical theology and to abandon the subject-object schema. Since Kant, God-language has lost its ontological roots, and it is impossible to make the God of practical reason into an objective reality.[10]

For Barth, God is the basis of his own objectivity in so far as, through revelation, he gratuitously becomes an object of knowledge and love. For Bultmann, the objectification of God in the metaphysical form of traditional theology is the same procedure as that of mythical thought, which would control God by talking of the beyond in the categories of this world. Any objective language about God is necessarily idolatrous because we cannot speak of God beyond what reaches us here and now in the decision of faith. The only way in which I can respect God's objectivity is to allow myself to be transformed by him in the obedience of faith instead of making him present to me as a represented object.

This desire to go beyond the objectivism of traditional theology is common to many present-day developments in theology, whether in so-called existentialist theology or in theological personalism. But, in the light of the fate of metaphysics, we may ask if this attack on the objectivity of God is not secretly related to the same enterprise of metaphysical theology, its desire for explanations. Put another way, is not this trend in theology, which is trying to come to terms with the irreducible event of revelation by starting from man defined as existence instead of from man defined as a rational animal, itself still to some extent dominated by the subjectivity of man?

In the face of this tendency of non-metaphysical theology, it is sometimes rightly asked whether God is still known in himself. If we speak of God in terms of a call, surely we reduce him to the pure paradox of a confrontation with man? If God is reduced to the occurrence of an encounter which changes me, the content of God is of little importance; he still has his regulative function. We have replaced the God of metaphysics by the God of the ethical conscience: God understood as absolute demands and the regulating principle of human action. We may therefore put the question: When theological existentialism no longer dares to objectify God in order to preserve his inexpressible character, does it not reduce God to the meaning he has for man? If this is so, existentialist theology, trying to be non-metaphysical in order the better to respect the particular originality of the God of faith, is in fact evidence for the anthropological orientation of theology in modern times. We are witnessing the end of the existentialization and interiorization of the faith which began with Luther and in which Feuerbach saw an "anthropocentric" shift.[11] It is also significant that in Catholicism and Protestantism today there is a reaction against the idealism and individualism of existentialist hermeneutics, and a new emphasis on the historical basis of Christianity. The new theologies of history (Moltmann and, especially, Pannenberg) reject a starting-point for the search for God in the immanence of thought, and look for a hermeneutic criterion in universal history, seen as the revelation of God.

An accurate description of the real situation of contemporary theology in its role as talk about God would seem to be given in the following question: At the moment when the God-concept, the object of traditional metaphysics, is dead, how can we overcome theological objectivism without falling into the anthropocentrism of existentialist theologies? To conclude, I would simply like to suggest the most promising directions for a non-metaphysical Christian theology which would retain its speculative ambitions.

IV
THE NON-METAPHYSICAL THEOLOGY OF THE FUTURE

Theology as the science of faith must work out its own way of handling concepts. It is concerned with an historical revelation which is accessible only in faith and has at its disposal a certain number of basic concepts with an essential relation to the historical event of salvation. The appropriation of these basic concepts by the understanding is, however, never complete. The permanent task of theology as an attempt to understand faith will be to work out a new language always based on the basic concepts of revelation but trying to go beyond them in an effort to make the content of faith more intelligible at a given moment of history. Since the realities of faith are by definition accessible only through an interpretation, the language of theology will inevitably be a speculative language in the sense that it goes beyond the limits of descriptive language. In its effort to work out a new speculative language, Christian theology will make privileged use of the resources of philosophical language, but it is not tied to any specific conceptual system. Even if theology cannot abandon the ontological content of its statements, it is free in relation to the categories and movement of thought of traditional metaphysics.

It is this freedom which the theology of the future is trying to demonstrate by its claim to be non-metaphysical. Christian theology today is trying to escape from the double impasse of theological objectivism and theological existentialism which we have discussed. The third way must be that of a non-objectifying speculative theology which can escape from the destiny of metaphysics as seen by Heidegger. Theology cannot abandon its speculative and systematic ambitions, but it must be able to use its freedom to say what it has been given to say by revelation. A theology which abandons the movement of thought within metaphysical thought will not try to objectify God by identifying him with the supreme Being, the basis of all existence. But for all that God is not a pure "It," and not the other party without content in an encounter about which nothing can be said. In this search for a non-objectifying ontological language the theologian can find extremely valuable philosophical material in the later Heidegger's "ontology of language," and in particular in his meditation on "saying as a part of being" or, better, "being's claim on saying."[12] "What language says is not necessarily the formulation of propositions *about* objects. In its depths language is the expression of what reveals itself and addresses itself to man in many ways, to the extent that man does not close himself to what is disclosed by means of the dominion of objectifying thought and by restricting himself to this."[13]

Heidegger himself would reject any use of his philosophy in theology, but we may ask, following Ott, if it is not possible to re-examine the relation of theological thought to revelation in the light of the new questioning of being which Heidegger initiated. Just as there is a "topology of being," or a special place where the truth of being is disclosed, there is also a special place in which the truth which is the source of revelation allows itself to be appropriated by the believer. Our task therefore must be to begin a movement of thought in theology which will appropriate revealed truth by starting from its special place instead of trying to explain the irreducible mystery of God by starting from a pre-existing basis, whether it is God as Absolute Being or man in his self-understanding.[14] The privileged place for talk about God is the economy of the incarnate Word. We cannot start from an existing idea of God and then see how it is modified by the event of the incarnation. We can only know the God of Jesus Christ by starting from the particular history of Jesus. The Christian God is not an "object" in the sense of a *Gegenstand*, something which can be controlled. He has the objectivity of a personal mystery. If non-metaphysical theology is faithful to the place which is our starting-point in appropriating the truth of revelation, it will go beyond not only the subject-object schema but the representative schema of an interpersonal "I-Thou" relation between man and God.

Non-metaphysical theology, rooted in the economy, will continue to conceive of God as being, but no longer in the categories of idea, substance and nature. It will think of him in the categories of history and eschatology, and will try in this way to express the ontological primacy of the future over the present in the divine Being. Eternity will now no longer be a negative property, the absence of time; it will describe God's control over the future. If the future is the mode of being most appropriate to the biblical God, we can see that he cannot be captured by the objectifications of theism, and that no event in the history of salvation (not even the resurrection of Christ) can exhaust his promises. The truth of talk about God will be much more gradual anticipation and manifestation than *adaequatio* in relation to an immutable essence. And history is less the epiphany through time of the eternal presence of God than the gradual accomplishment of a future which is always unknown and will not be disclosed until the end of history, but opens each present moment on to the future.

We can now see that non-metaphysical theology is not just one more anti-philosophical slogan. It is the demand for a theology which will at last be "theological." The theology of the future will still be an ontological theology, but will aim at being a *theology of reality*. Going beyond the metaphysical dualism of God and the world, it will have to work towards a better understanding of how Jesus Christ is the unity of the reality of God and the reality of the world.

4. From the Theologies of the Word to the Theology of History

We are observing today a growing interest in the *theology of history* which is tending to take the place of *theologies of the word*. This is not only true of evangelical theology in which the revaluation of history among authors such as Wolfhart Pannenberg and Jürgen Moltmann is consistent with an expressed desire to go beyond the anti-liberal problematics of Barth and Bultmann. This is also true of Catholic theology in which the program of "political theology," which has Johannes Baptist Metz as its main inspiration, is explicitly moving away from the transcendental theology of Karl Rahner.

It could be justly reiterated that Judaeo-Christian revelation is inseparably word and history. God reveals himself *in* and *through* history. But as Barth was already asking, the essential question is to know whether revelation is a "predicate of history," or whether it is history which must be understood as a predicate of revelation. For Barth—and this is also true in another sense for Bultmann—history is a predicate of revelation. Among authors like Pannenberg, we are witnessing a complete turnabout: It is revelation which is becoming a predicate of history. *Revelation as history* was the keynote of the theologians and exegetes gathered around Pannenberg.[1]

Theology of the word or theology of history? Behind these two possible interpretations of Christianity lies a fascinating theological debate which concerns the very future of Christianity in its confrontation with modern culture in this second half of the twentieth century. We would simply like to show in this chapter that the transition from a theology of the word to a theology of history is governed by different hermeneutical choices. And these differing horizons of interpretation in terms of which the Christian message is reinterpreted are inseparable from the historicity of man and his understanding of himself and the world. This is the precise manner in which the hermeneutical problem is being posed for us today. This in turn forces us to question the theologies of the word to the extent that they are overly "authoritarian" and insufficiently historical.

The Hermeneutical Question

Christian revelation does not primarily consist in the unveiling of a certain number of truths about God and about man, or about the religious attitude that man should have toward God, but in the historical event of Jesus Christ. Now, in what way does Jesus Christ concern us today? The whole hermeneutical question has its roots in the attempt to overcome the difference between the present and the past without canceling it out. The task of hermeneutics will be to reproduce what happened for the first witnesses of the Word of God, namely the encounter with the reality of God in the reality of the world and our own lives, in such a way that the Word of God becomes contemporary for us at its very springing forth. In order to accomplish this task of actualization, theology as hermeneutics is becoming more and more aware of a double historical distance, not only the distance between the past event of revelation and the present of our culture, but also of the distance between the scriptural accounts and the historical events themselves (cf. *supra*, p. 44).

Pannenberg explains this new situation of theology very well in his study on the *Crisis of the Scripture Principle:* "The gulf between fact and significance, between the history of Jesus and the multiplicity of New Testament witnesses to him, marks one side of present theological research. On the other side is the equally deep gulf between the cultural world of the New Testament texts and that of our own present age. . . . It is with this problem of the 're-iteration' (*Wiederholung*) of the same content in a completely changed situation that modern hermeneutics deals."[2]

As soon as the literal meaning Scripture no longer coincides with its historical content, we can no longer be satisfied with a theology which rests only on the authority of Scripture or of the Word of God. Scripture, certainly, remains the soul of all theology, but less as a *given* directly inspired by God than as a *witness* which only surrenders its meaning when grasped within the evolution of historical tradition.

Historico-critical research has even forced Protestant theology to question the principle dear to Luther, concerning the autonomous authority of Scripture. But this "depositivizing" (*Entpositivierung*)[3], to take up a key word of Pannenberg's theological program, is consistent with the modern rule of reason which does not agree to submit to any truth in the name of an authority, even God's. Modern man can only break loose from *suspicion* if the affirmation which is claimed brings with it the proof of its own truth. The question which is asked today is that of "a revelation of the divinity which is not only affirmed, but which is convincing in itself."[4]

Moreover, some people often conclude too quickly that there is an irreconcilable divorce between the attitude of faith and modern reason's rule of autonomy. This would be to forget that Christian faith only encounters the revealed God in history. Christianity is not a myth or a gnosis; it is the expression of a faith founded on something historical. While the theologies of the Word have taken refuge in the supernaturalism of a hypostasized Word of God or in the subjectivity of the believer, there is today a whole theological current which is striving to restore the value of history as the only means of speaking a language that modern man can understand. It is the historical fact itself which becomes the hermeneutical principle of theology. This rejection of an "authoritarian" theology and this attempt to get back to the historical event beyond the kerygma are consistent with both the nature of contemporary hermeneutics and the status of reason in our present-day culture. Besides, this necessary mediation of history insures the objectivity of the faith and shelters it from the illusions of religious consciousness. It is the *historical difference* of a past event which is not readily at the disposal of the faith that guarantees the objective character of this faith.

The Limitations of the Theologies of the Word

It would be difficult to speak of theology of history in reference to the two great theological works of the first half of the twentieth century: Barth and Bultmann. They are both essentially theologies of the word. Despite their respective differences, the starting point common to both Barth and Bultmann is to believe that "historico-critical research as scientific observation leaves no room for the salvation event."[5] Against the liberalism which dissolves faith and revelation, Barth and Bultmann center their theology on the *decision of faith* in response to the call of the Word of God. Barth insists on the actualization of the Word of God in the present-day preaching of the Church. For Bultmann, it is on account of the kerygma that the events of the history of salvation become saving events for man today. As saving, these events are only accessible to faith and do not yield themselves to historical research.[6]

Neither of the two, according to Pannenberg, has really grounded revelation in history. Barth would shelter revelation from historical observation by appealing to the supra-historical kernel of the faith, to the Incarnation as *Urgeschichte*. Bultmann, on the other hand, noting the impossibility of producing a history of Jesus, wants to save the cross as kerygma, as an event for us today. To overcome the historical distance between the primitive kerygma and man today, he devotes himself to undertaking a demythologizing of the kerygma and to looking for the essence of the message according to the existential possibilities of man. But, in fact, he dissolves history in man's historicity.[7]

It is then apparent that a whole current of recent German theology seeks to get back to the event beyond the kerygma. This was already the trend of the new hermeneutics of Bultmann's followers, Ernst Fuchs and Gerhard Ebeling, who lean toward a grasp of history based on a study of language as an event of being, along the lines of the second Heidegger. We have been able to rightly speak about these theological attempts at "theologies of existence," to the extent that it is a matter of "enlightenment opening itself to God in the process of human existence." Human existence remains the starting point, and the decisive hermeneutical principle remains, as with Bultmann, the existentialist *Fraglichkeit* ("questionableness"), namely human existence as a question of God. For Pannenberg and his school, if you start with human existence and if you immediately identify the question of man with the question about God, you fall back into subjectivism and individualism. The only starting point which can guarantee the objectivity of the faith is its *historical otherness*. To account for the coming of God into history, we should not invoke a "supra-history" as does Barth or a "history of salvation" as distinct from secular history as does Cullmann. Only universal *history* furnishes a horizon for comprehension that is adequate to account for the particular events which ground the Christian faith. "History is the most all-encompassing horizon of Christian theology."[9] In other words, we must refuse to identify hermeneutics with an understanding of language as has been the case for the theologies of existence since Bultmann. Behind the language are the *facts* which give meaning. Moreover, the historical method should also be the method of Christian theology, since there is only one single historical method and one single body of historical knowledge.

Hermeneutics and History

As we have already suggested, the recent questioning of the value of the theologies of the word or of existence and the new favor which the theology of history is enjoying are directly connected with the hermeneutical problem. Since Kant, theologians have accepted without question an historical method which separates facts from their interpretation. Indeed it was necessary to take shelter from the historical criticism concerning the life of

Jesus. Starting with the Kantian distinction between *sein* and *sollen*, the neo-Kantians established a separation between *fact* (object of the experimental sciences) and *meaning* (object of any ethics or metaphysics). This separation ended up in empirical positivism and the positivism of freedom. Christian theology, in order to escape the damaging consequences of historicism, reacted by reinforcing the supernatural authority of the Word of God without resorting to the criterion of history.

Seen in this light, it is not surprising that theology gradually lost its universality. The proper sphere of theology then shrinks to the inaccessible and unverifiable sphere of the supernatural, and theology is supposed to give up any possibility of dialogue with the other disciplines of the mind. In modern times this isolation of theology could be noted both in Protestant theology's attachment to the old-style scriptural positivism and in Catholic theology's submission to an inflated authority of the Magisterium. Furthermore, the result was a ruinous distinction between the task of the exegete-historian and that of the hermeneutical theologian. The exegete-historian looks for the meaning of the event from its historical context while the hermeneutical theologian strives to make the meaning of the past event present for us today. These are the two modes of understanding to which we must connect the all too famous opposition between the Jesus of history and the Christ of faith, *Historie* and *Geschichte*.[10]

Pannenberg's great merit is to have shown that a theology of history is only possible if we can overcome the opposition between fact and meaning on the level of historical knowledge. His solution consists in seeking within universal history the reconciliation of historico-critical knowledge and its interpretation.

An event only has meaning in the context of history. We cannot stand outside of history by appealing to an interpretation coming from outside, since the actualization of the meaning cannot be separated from its historical coming to be. In this way Pannenberg goes beyond the Kantian heritage and joins the line of Hegel, who was the first to fight against the separation of fact and meaning.

In his important study, *Hermeneutic and Universal Histo-*

ry, Pannenberg seeks to clarify his own position relative to the history of modern hermeneutics in its constant effort to overcome the historical difference between the past and the present. He begins by getting away from the *psychological* conception of hermeneutics in Scheiermacher and Dilthey. For these last two the relationship between the past and the present is already determined in advance. "Indeed, the fact that life and the possibilities of life are identical for the interpreter as well as for the man in the past is the *a priori* link between the present and the past being interpreted."[11] Thus, by *a priori* restricting the question raised in the text to the possibilities of human beings, they can by-pass the singularity of the past event and subordinate its meaning to the possibilities of man today. History, in its irreducibility, is dissolved in man's historicity.

Bultmann, in his interpretation of the New Testament, basically sets up the problem in the same way. He *a priori* restricts the meaning of past events to modern man's understanding of himself. On the contrary, we must respect the otherness of the past event which calls forth a response from us today in its very difference. While the writings of the New Testament also deal primarily with God and his action in the events of the world and its history, this being what determines what they have to say about man, Bultmann goes about it backward. "One must grasp affirmations about God, the world and history as simple *expressions* based on a human understanding of existence."[12]

In the *Hermeneutics of Language* of Fuchs and Ebeling, interpretation and history still remain separated. It was not until Gadamer and his work *Wahrheit und Methode* (1960) that we find a close interpenetration of the summons of the text itself and its present understanding. Pannenberg considers that Gadamer succeeds in taking a decisive step forward in the clarification of the hermeneutical problem insofar as he really takes the *historical difference* between the present and the past seriously.

"(In Gadamer) it is a matter of keeping in view, without prior restrictions, the claim laid upon the bearer, reader, observer, or interpreter, as the actual center of the hermeneutical theme. For precisely this reason, Gadamer struggles to maintain without effacement the difference between the historical situation of the text to be interpreted and the interpreter's present era. For it is just this difference that articulates the claim the text makes upon contemporary understanding. Thus, hermeneutical and historical motifs, in the narrower sense, interpenetrate in Gadamer's thought. In this case, historical difference acquires decisive significance for the structure of the process of understanding itself."[13]

Contrary to what happens in existential hermeneutics, the hermeneutical task for Gadamer does not consist in wiping out the difference, but in first enhancing it to the fullest. Understanding will consist in a "fusion of horizons" (*Horizontverschmelzung*), namely the elaboration of a wider horizon from the horizon of the text and the interpreter's horizon.

But if Pannenberg admits to seeing in the hermeneutical understanding a "language event" (*Sprachvorgang*), he disagrees with Gadamer's comparison of interpretation to a dialogue. The text is not really a "you" which speaks to us; it is incapable of speaking. If we can speak of a *language event* in the case of interpretation, it is not because a dialogue could take place between the reader and the text to be interpreted, but because the reader has to invent a new language to understand the text. "The fusion of horizons is not primarily a product of language, but rather the invention of a new manner of speaking, an expression of the fusion of horizons which is accomplished through understanding."[14]

By comparing interpretation to a dialogue and appealing to something "unsaid" in the text to be interpreted, Gadamer still does not surmount the opposition between the objective truth of the statement and the subjectivity of the one who interprets it. For Pannenberg "the text does not speak, rather the interpreter finds an expression of language which synthesizes the reality presented by the text with his own present horizon."[15] But to ascribe to the Word not only the sense of the text but the sense of the reality it speaks of, universal history itself must be taken as the horizon for interpreting the text. Only universal history can mediate the meaning of the past in relation to the present without canceling out their differences. "It is only in connection with the universal history that the 'in those days' of the text can be joined to the 'today' of the interpreter in such a way that their temporal and historical difference is not erased, but rather is preserved and yet transcended in the context of the events that link them one to another."[16]

So, for Pannenberg, who always seeks to overcome any ruinous separation between fact and meaning, the meaning of a past event is immanent to the event itself, even in the case of a provisional meaning which is constantly revised by new events. Only at the end of history can the event unveil its final meaning. We cannot step outside of history, since the actualization of the meaning is inseparable from its historical coming to be. According to I. Berten's apt formulation, "history is its own interpreter."[17]

But for all this we do not end up with the Hegelian solution of an absolute knowledge of the contingent from the totality of history. Indeed the end of history has not yet arrived. However, we can have a provisional knowledge of the end of history, since it is anticipated in Jesus Christ. Even while seeking the mediation of the present with past history in universal history, Pannenberg therefore maintains the openness of our knowledge to the future and acknowledges thereby the finite quality of our knowledge. In regard to what separates Gadamer from Hegel, he states: "Our here and now situation, namely finitude as the vantage point of thought and openness to the future, makes any simple repetition of the Hegelian system impossible."[18]

Universal History as a Hermeneutical Principle

Pannenberg's aim is then to elaborate a theology of history, taking as a hermeneutical principle universal history. The proper area for theology is history itself, but considered eschatologically. We have seen how much importance he attaches to the historical difference between the past and the present. But this difference is inseparable from the *eschatological* difference between the world as historical totality and the God who unveils himself in it.

The starting point for this theology of history is not, as in the theologies of the word, the question of God asked from human existence's "being in question." It is rather the proof of God, starting with the world considered as an historical totality. In other words, it is the historical method which poses the question of God and discovers his revelation. If indeed the object of Christian faith is the historical revelation of God in Jesus Christ, the object of the faith must be able to hinge upon the historical method. What distinguishes the theology of universal history is not the method it uses, only the object studied. In contrast to theologians who insist on the decision of faith, Pannenberg goes so far as to speak of an "evident quality" of the revelation of God in history even for those who do not have the faith. He branches off from Cullmann, with whom he still shares a similar sense of revelation as history, because Cullmann sets up a *qualitative difference* between the events of secular history and those of the history of salvation which are only accessible to faith. "Such a theology of history is distinguished from this sort of salvation history in that it seeks to be historically verifiable."[19]

We can only understand such a radical attitude which scandalized several of Pannenberg's critics in reference to his theses on the indirect revelation of God and on Christ as the anticipation of the end of history.

In contrast to the idea of "self-revelation" of God which has been current in theology since Hegel, what strikes us about the Jewish conception of revelation is its indirect character. "The revelation of God Himself, according to the Biblical accounts, was not accomplished in the manner of a theophany, but indirectly by historical acts of God."[20] The events precisely as acts of God indirectly reveal to us something about God. And the Word, in the sense of an inspiration, does not come in to complete history as revelation. "This would be a return to a pretension of authoritarian-type revelation."[21] A particular event manifests its meaning in its relationship and its difference with other events, which is to say ultimately with the "history of tradition."

But since a particular event as an act of God can only furnish a partial revelation of God, the full self-revelation of God is only possible when the totality of history is regarded as revelation. This ultimate meaning of history can only be revealed at the end of history. For Hegel, history is a theophany of God because history is a totality already completed. But Pannenberg does not deduce God from any totalization of history (a criticism directed against him by Moltmann). Even though history has not been completed, history is revelation of God because the end of history is *anticipated* in the destiny of Jesus of Nazareth and more particularly in the event of the resurrection. In the resurrection of Christ as the "prolepsis" of the end of history, we have the key to universal history. In this way he replies to the question of Lessing and Strauss: How can a particular event have an absolute significance as revelation from God?

However, even though the revelation of God in Jesus Christ is definitive, we still do not have a full knowledge of God. If it is true that a particular event can only manifest its whole meaning at the end of history, this is also true of the Christ event itself. "We do not yet have definitive knowledge of what really happened in the ministry and destiny of Jesus. But this reservation itself belongs to the ultimacy of that event. It was the only way possible, in the midst of the historical relativity of ongoing time and of the knowledge which is bound to it, for knowledge of the meaning warranted by the destiny of Jesus to remain nondefinitive."[22] Pannenberg, while speaking of anticipating the end of history, therefore respects the finite and temporary character of our knowledge of history and leaves the future open to a possible unexpected. We must hold on to both the provisional and the definitive character of revelation. We are between the "already" and the "not yet." Moreover, this paradox of the "already" and the "not yet" should be placed in objective history and not only in the subjective experience of the Christian.

So, precisely as Pannenberg appeals to Hegel by choosing universal history as a hermeneutical criterion, he rejects the idea of absolute knowledge by stating that the meaning is only anticipated as long as history remains incomplete. He attempts to preserve in an eschatological perspective the *newness* of history. History does repeat bygone events but never without bringing in something new. God's presence in history must be regarded as the presence of the future in the present, as what enables the future to be open and not closed in on itself, and not as the presence of eternity in time. History is constantly straining toward its fulfillment, but it cannot fulfill itself. It is the end event, the resurrection of Jesus, which repeats and takes up again (*Wiederholung* means both repetition and taking up again) all of history to give it its full completion. It is therefore a free act of God which completes history and gives it its meaning. "Left to itself, history is contingency deprived of meaning, a failure; outside of the revelation of salvation in Jesus Christ (and the ultimate revelation at the *eschaton*), history itself is by no means, any more than man in himself, reference to God. History is pure question without an answer (and that is why there is no way of analogy which enables us to cross over from the world to God)."[23]

It must be admitted that this recognition of the contingency of history which can only take its meaning from its end seems to contradict Pannenberg's thesis about the universal character of revelation "which is open to any man who has eyes to see."

I do not wish to approach the tremendously delicate question of the relationship between *faith* and *reason* in Pannenberg here. By dint of wanting to avoid the subjectivism of an irrational decision of faith, does not Pannenberg reduce the faith to historical knowledge? He insistently replies that while historical research is for him the indispensable foundation of faith, it never brings absolute certitude. Faith draws its certainty only from the unconditional act by which the believer relies on God for his salvation. "The mere knowledge of God's revelation does not yet mean participation in the salvation contained in that message of revelation. It is only when man abandons himself to this revelation, when he commits himself with trust to this event that he receives his share in it."[24]

On the other hand it must be clearly understood that Pannenberg rightly intends to get beyond the opposition of faith and reason as we find it in traditional theology. Reason for him is essentially historical reason, which is to say not an *a priori* faculty, but a reflection which moves forward by steps and recognizes the difference which separates it from its object, namely the totality of history. Thus, truth is not so much adequation to some immutable essence on the level of thought as it is an anticipation of a future reality. If we reject the Hegelian idea of reflection which culminates in the concept, then faith and reason are no longer opposed. In the same way that faith is knowledge turned toward the future, straining toward the eschatological realization, so reason is an anticipatory knowledge which becomes conscious of its inadequacy in relation to the reality in its totality which is history. The unity of faith and reason will be realized only at the end of history which will coincide with the full revelation of the meaning of history. Meanwhile, theology is rightly defined as the effort of the believing intelligence to anticipate the eschatological unity of faith and reason. That is why Pannenberg thinks that the theology of history should extend into a "theology of reason."[25]

Interpretation or Transformation of History?

We have seen how the overtaking of existential hermeneutics and of the new hermeneutics of language by a hermeneutical conception which resolutely chooses universal history as its horizon of interpretation accounts for the transition from the theologies of the word to the theology of history. In the face of "authoritarian" theologies which hypostasize the Word of God[26] and insist in a unilateral fashion on the instant decision of the act of faith, it is foremost a matter of demonstrating for the sake of modern man the credibility of Christianity as revelation of God in the language of facts. Pannenberg's theology of history is intended to be an interpretation of the meaning of universal history, starting with the end of history anticipated in Jesus Christ.

But today, confronted with the secular ideologies of the future, theology cannot be satisfied with proposing a different interpretation of history. It should manifest the historical efficacy of Christianity for the transformation of history and of man in their social and political dimensions. This is the sense of Moltmann's theology of hope and J.B. Metz' political theology. "The theologian therefore is not content to give a different interpretation to the world, history and the human condition; for him it is a matter of transforming them while awaiting the divine transformation."[27]

We know that Moltmann rightly criticizes Pannenberg for having abandoned the "promise-fulfillment" structure in favor of the "history of traditions" as the hermeneutical key to the theology of history. In fact, his theology of universal history would only be a return to and an enlargement upon the Greek theology of the cosmos. "The cosmological proof for the existence of God, which by arguing from reality as cosmos to the single divine *arche* would give proof of a cosmological monotheism, has been replaced by a theology of history which, following a similar line of reasoning, argues from the unity of reality as history to the one God."[28]

Basically it would still be a question of the world as the "epiphany" of God, even if the totality of history has been substituted for the cosmos. Certainly history still remains open to the future and it can only achieve a provisional knowledge of God so long as it has not been completed. However, in spite of this eschatological coefficient, Pannenberg's theology would remain dependent on thought patterns from the Greek theology of the cosmos. "But if history becomes a new concept for the 'universe' or for 'reality in its totality' then this is to coin a new concept of the cosmos and no longer take a 'historic' view of history."[29] Pannenberg's theology is still moving in the "apocalyptic" horizon for interpreting the totality of reality. This is not the "horizon of the transformation of the world," the only one adequate to the biblical conception of history. In other words, revelation in Pannenberg remains under the sign of the *logos*; it still does not have the character of a *promise*.

Pannenberg has replied at length to Moltmann's objections.[30] He has no trouble showing that for him history is not something static which would point back to God in the manner of the cosmos: It is the very action of God, and this is how it is indirect revelation of God. I would like to think that Pannenberg and Moltmann's starting points are less far apart than Moltmann would like to admit, but I do not want to get into the debate here. I would only like to emphasize in concluding the import and the timeliness of the trend manifested in Moltmann's theology of history.

Pannenberg's theology is a reinterpretation of Christianity, starting with history taken as a totality, and some have not been reluctant to speak of it as "Christian Hegelianism." As we will see in the following chapter, Moltmann's theology is a reinterpretation of Christianity from the notion of *future*. The future theme is not one among others but rather the only one which can account for the originality of Christianity which encounters God, not as an eternal God present in a history which repeats itself, but as God of the promises that arise from the future.

This theology of hope, which is both political and prophetic, leads to a "hermeneutics of mission," that is to say an interpretation of the biblical witnesses in the frame of a "history of mission." Theology cannot be satisfied with giving a theoretical interpretation of history; it has to lead to a *praxis*, a practical application, a transformation of the present in the name of the future. Indeed, if Christian faith is essentially faith in the resurrection as the event prophetic of the end of history, it is inseparable from the acting out of the mission of the Church as the actualization of this anticipation of the end of history.

We can guess without any difficulty the timeliness of such a theology of history at a time when so many ideologies or prospective sciences are striving to gain control of the future of man. Christian theology aspires to be more than a science of interpretation. By choosing the *future* as a hermeneutical criterion, theology is becoming a "science of hope," which means eminently practical, an interpretation of Christian action as openness to the future, to the new, to the unforeseen.

The task of any theology of history will always be to keep the culmination of history beyond itself. Today, confronted with idolatrous and totalitarian conceptions of history, the irreplaceable function of Christian hope is to open up "a free field for the playing out of history."[31] Hope will necessarily encounter contradiction, since it must question scientific and technical millenarianisms as well as refuse to consecrate any established order.

Hope simply seeks to work effectively in the social promotion of human freedom. And those who might criticize such a theological trend for reducing Christianity to its social usefulness must be reminded that the future opened up by Christian hope is precisely the future of God, which implies an unforeseen and unsettling future. "The dialogue with a humanism which aspires to a 'future without God' may be able to encourage some Christians to give up looking for a 'God without His future.' "[32]

5. The Political Dimension of Christian Hope

Theology is often a good indicator of what the Church is living through in any given historical moment. We speak a lot today about "theology of history," "theology of the world," "theology of secularization," "political theology," "theology of revolution," "theology of development." It is as though at a time when the Church is increasingly on the fringes of today's society, it were becoming more acutely aware of its historical responsibility in regard to the future of man and the transformation of our societies.

Among these various theological attempts which seek to emphasize the historical responsibility of Christianity, we will especially single out, as particularly significant of a new orientation in Christian theology, two theological programs which came out of Germany: the "theology of hope" of the Protestant Jurgen Moltmann[1] and the "political theology" of Johannes Baptist Metz.[2]

These are theologies which insist, each in its own manner, on the *social* and *political* dimension of the Christian faith. We could point out in this a temptation to recover at any cost an audience in a world which gets along quite well without the Church. But, in fact, they are original reinterpretations of the Christian message which, by reason of a civilization affected by "future shock," are seeking to take the *eschatological* dimension of Christianity seriously. And in contrast to politicized theologies in which some see the expression of a "leftist neo-clericalism," they refrain from leading into detailed plans of action. They refuse to "sacralize" this or that theory of society or any particular determined political program. They run the risk of disillusioning those who primarily expect theology to legitimize this or that kind of commitment. The goal of theology is not to provide us with recipes, but to obtain for us a renewed understanding of Christianity in view of new questions raised by a changing world. It is quite clear that with the diversity and complexity of situations, any Christian theology which would be only the justification of the practice of one or another particular Christian group or of any local Church, would chance falling into ideology.

I

MOLTMANN'S THEOLOGY OF HOPE

In order to understand the theology of hope of Moltmann you must read it as a *theology of history* elaborated from the notion of *future*. It is a theology that wants to get away from both Karl Barth's *theology of the word* and Rudolf Bultmann's *theology of existence*. The common shortcoming to both of these theologies is not really taking seriously the eschatological dimension of Christianity. They both turn the eschatological reality into an *already here*, eternally present, instead of manifesting the operative force of the future promised by God for present history.

As the subtitle of his book indicates, Moltmann sets about studying "the foundations and the consequences of a Christian eschatology." The discovery of the eschatological message of Christianity already goes back more than sixty years. But within Protestant theology Moltmann considers himself to be the first to attempt a systematic reflection on the implications of eschatology for the understanding of Christian being and acting in the world. To accomplish this task, he readily appeals to the reflections on the concepts of *future* and *novelty* of the Marxist philosopher E. Bloch in his book *The Hope Principle*.

The Future as the Central Theme of Christianity

All through his book, Moltmann strives to demonstrate the radical link between eschatology and history. History is eschatological and eschatology is historical. Otherwise, we end up in a divorce between the faith increasingly relegated to the private sphere and a world left to its own movement as well as to the grasp of man's technological power. Religious subjectivism and scientific positivism have the same origin—an eschatologization of the faith which has lost its roots in the world and history.

The only way to respect the eschatological dimension of Christianity without short-circuiting history is to rediscover the original conception of history proper to the biblical tradition, which means a history for which the *future* is a privileged category. "The true category of history is no longer the past and the transient, but the *future*. The perception and interpretation of past history is then no longer archeological but eschatological and future-oriented" (p. 260). As Moltmann further says: "There is only one real problem in Christian theology: it is posed to theology by its object and through theology to humanity and human thought; that is the problem of the future" (p. 24).

This passion for the future which expresses itself in almost lyric terms enlivens from within Moltmann's rigorous and sometimes academic analyses and explains to a large degree the success of his book. Our cultural world is certainly under the sign of the future, whether this future fascinates us or whether it frightens us. The future is therefore going to provide the key for interpreting Scripture, and it is because Christian theology is entirely centered on the future that it is essentially a theology of hope. Hope is what gives an historical dimension to faith and a political dimension to love.

Moltmann really puts eschatology in its true place, in the ultimate future, but in such a way that it may influence the course of history and may invest the whole life of believers. A theology of hope which accepts the full implications of biblical eschatology ought to be equipped to overcome the divorce between faith and involvement in the world, between the world of God and the world of men, between theory and practice. Such is at least Moltmann's deep conviction.

The God "Ahead"

In the footsteps of many others, Moltmann devotes himself to showing what distinguishes biblical thought from Greek thought, in particular concerning the way history is experienced and the conception of God. But he is original inasmuch as he locates the break between the pagan religions and the religion of Israel in the difference between *epiphany* and *promise.* It is because the religion of Israel is a religion of promise that it creates the conditions for the possibility of an historical experience of reality. History determined by the promise does not consist in the "eternal return" as in the Greek conception, but is oriented toward the promised fulfillment.

The promises of the Old Testament are specific, insofar as the history of Israel never rendered the promises fruitless, whether they remain unfulfilled or whether they are fulfilled and no longer reserve a future. Let us say that God, as God of the promise, remains above all the fulfillments; he does not exhaust the promises in any historical reality. The future therefore always remains open.

By pushing to its ultimate implications the "promise-fulfillment" dialectic as the key to interpreting the history of Israel, Moltmann invites us to re-think the relationship between God and history and the most specific attribute of God himself. The relationship between God and history must not be interpreted according to the dialectic of the fleeting moment and the eternal present of God, or the dialectic of the present and the future. In the perspective of the cyclical time of the Greeks, historical events are passing and successive events which reflect in their manner the eternal immutability of God. History for the Greeks is a universe of changing and variable epiphanies of the eternal present. "History for Jews and Christians means history of salvation, the divine history of the promise. The 'Divine' is not contemplated as Perpetual Being, in permanent and subsisting orders and in patterns which are repeated. Rather the 'Divine' is awaited from the God of the promises as arising from the future" (p. 260).

History is therefore always open to something new and

God, as God of the promises, is the master of an unforeseeable future. In order to better underscore the originality of the biblical God in its difference from the Eternal Present of Parmenides or the Unmoved Mover of Aristotle, Moltmann readily echoes E. Bloch in saying that "God by the nature of His being is situated in the future." This would be a manner of understanding the mysterious reply of God to Moses in Exodus, chapter 3: "I will be who I will be." It is really the history of the promise in Israel that says who he is. The God of Israel is not the God "above"; he is the God "ahead." He is not locatable in history or in the subjectivity of the believer; he is only *promised* and only hope which is always ready to go beyond itself can meet him.

The Future of Jesus Christ

By interpreting the resurrection of Christ in the context of the Jewish theology of the promise, Moltmann founds a *theology of history* which is intended to be at the same time a *political theology*. While all too often the resurrection of Christ is understood as the fulfillment of the promise which puts an end to history, Moltmann devotes himself to showing that the coming of Christ has not exhausted the promise, because the resurrection points us toward a future. Actually, it does not refer us to an epiphanic God, to the God who is, but to the God who is coming.

There is no doubt that the resurrection of Christ already fulfills—in an anticipated way—the promise of God. However, it is not yet the final fulfillment. "The Resurrection is not an event which closes by fulfilling the promise, but an event which opens because it re-enforces the promise by bearing it out."[3] Consistent with the central thesis of his book on the religion of Israel as the religion of the promise, Moltmann is more sensitive to the "not yet" of the resurrection than to the "already here." That is why the return of Christ in the Parousia will not be merely the *unveiling* of what has already occurred in a hidden fashion, but will be the final fulfillment.

It is therefore legitimate to designate the Mystery of the Parousia as the "future of Jesus Christ." "The object of Christian expectation is none other than the Christ who has come, but something new is expected of him which has not yet come to pass so far. Christians await the fulfillment in all things of the promised justice of God, the fulfillment of the resurrection of the dead promised in His Resurrection, and the fulfillment of the Lordship of the Crucified over all things, promised in his being lifted up in glory" (p. 229).

Thanks to this reinterpretation of the resurrection of Christ in the mode of the promise, Moltmann feels able to give to history after Christ its full meaning and to found the *political* dimension of Christian hope. The time of the Church is not only the time of the "remembrance" of the past event of the resurrection; it is rather the time of the progressive realization of the future possibilities contained in the resurrection: the annihilation of the nothingness of death and the reconciliation of man with himself, with others and with God. Thus the resurrection begets a real history, the history of men who protest the present in the name of the promised future. We can then speak of a real progress of the time of the Church. And this progress does not come from the time of the world which continues to run its course. It must rather be said that it is the resurrection with all its possibilities for the future that makes human reality *historic* and *progressive*.

Hope, according to Moltmann, is not only an expectation; it is the demand for an "historic transformation of life" (p. 330). It therefore has political import. Contrary to the opinion of some of his critics who find fault with Moltmann for not having shown the link between this concrete history in which we are struggling and the new humanity, the new world promised by God, his whole book is intended as a reaction against any eschatology conceived as a flight forward and seeks to make history the setting for the progressive fulfillment of the promises. Hope is like the "spear-point" of history, which questions the present to make the future present here and now. Christians are the witnesses to a promise which brings about something *brand new* in history, which gives it a possible future. The theology of hope opens out then on to a theology of the mission of the Church. This mission should really already anticipate here and now the possibilities for the future contained in the Jesus Christ event, he who cancelled out in his person the difference between the crucifixion and the resurrection.

A Community in Exodus

Moltmann's work concludes in a final chapter: "A Community in Exodus," which strives to spell out the responsibilities of the Christian community in modern society. The beautiful text of the epistle to the Hebrews 13:13 could serve as a hallmark for all of Moltmann's work: "Let us therefore go forth from the camp to him, carrying his disgrace; for we have no permanent city here below, but we seek the one which is to come." Despite its still abstract character, this last chapter would attempt to prove that the theology of hope is not a mere ideology, which after so many others proposes a new interpretation of history. The "science of hope" would seek to inaugurate a new joining of theory to practice. To interpret Christian acting from the standpoint of the future is to found an ethical practice capable of transforming history. Moltmann re-applies to himself as a theologian the eleventh thesis of Marx on Feuerbach: "The theologian therefore is not satisfied with providing a different interpretation of the world, history and the human condition; for him it is a matter of *transforming* them in the expectation of a divine transformation" (p. 84).

The mission of the Church, as an eschatological community, will be to call into question the *present* of society, whether it clings to the past or whether it abolishes history in its planning for the future. The theology of hope is neither reactionary nor exclusively progressive. It is of another order; it seeks to introduce into historical repetition a principle of newness: the active *difference* of hope. Christian hope will have a political dimension, which is to say that it will provoke in history significant anticipations of the future promised in Jesus Christ. It will make common cause with human hopes in view of a transformation of man and society, but while orienting them toward the eschatological future and therefore by relativizing their always ambivalent accomplishments.

Moltmann's position on the role of the Church is nuanced and could lend itself to misinterpretation. He refuses to make the Church the setting for the private salvation of individuals. But he does not want it to become a kind of mutual aid society which provides a spiritual breath of fresh air for an increasingly materialistic, technical and collectivistic world.

The Christian community in exodus in the world does not pretend to anticipate the Kingdom of God here and now by the sole fact of its social and political action. But in obedience to the promise, it discerns and prepares the way for the Kingdom. "The mission does not only consist in spreading faith and hope, but in promoting a historical transformation of life" (p. 330). One of Moltmann's major contributions in regard to our present questions on "faith and politics" and "Church and development" is to have shown that the eschatology of the New Testament transforms the promises of the Old Testament without abolishing them; these promises in turn announce a reconciliation of mankind in the scheme of history itself.

From this there results a widening of the notion of *salvation*; the following text well expresses the import of this development: "If we take seriously this prophetic and eschatological background against which the preaching of the Gospel by Christians emerges, the goal of the Christian mission must also become plain. It aims at reconciliation with God (2 Cor. 5:18ff), the forgiveness of sins and the abolition of godlessness. But salvation (*sôteria*) ought to be also understood in the sense of the Old Testament as the *shalom*. This does not mean merely salvation of the soul or rescue from an evil world, or merely comfort for the troubled conscience, but even more the realization of an eschatological hope for *justice*, the *humanization* of man, peace for all creation" (p. 329).

II
THE "POLITICAL" THEOLOGY OF METZ

The political theology of Johannes B. Metz, a Catholic theologian, professor at Münster and a former pupil of Karl Rahner, owes much to Moltmann's theology of hope. His program stems from the determination to get away from Bultmann's approach. At the same time he seeks to react against the "trend towards the private" in Christianity which was brought about by the anti-Church struggle at the time of the Enlightenment.

Because the "faith-politics" problem is such a burning issue within the Church in France today, we must immediately forestall any disappointment regarding Metz's political theology. Indeed, you should not look for a "politicized theology" in the sense of an immediate legitimizing of this or that kind of political involvement on the part of Christians. Often laymen ask the professional theologian to immediately justify in the name of the faith a particular form of political involvement. The political theology of Metz represents an attempt to respond to this very practical need on the part of Christians. However, he seeks to respond to this need in "critical" and not in immediate fashion. Moreover, any immediate theological justification of this or that kind of social or political action would run the risk of being just another ideology, which would not rest on any rigorous analysis of the concrete conditions for the liberation of man.

Neither should you look in the program of Metz for a theology of "politics" in the sense of an "area" theology such as the theology of "work" or the theology of "development." It is most precisely a *fundamental theology* or a theology which reflects in a critical manner on the social and political implications of the Christian faith. Let us say that political theology does not only consider man as a *moral* being, but as a *political* being in the most rigorous sense of the term. This means that he is an *historical* being who only fulfills his essence in a relationship to society. Man is only himself through the mediation of his political dimension. If "political" is what best defines the totality of human existence, a gap can no longer be maintained between faith and politics.

Certainly, the object of faith is God, which no utopia, no line of reason and therefore no kind of politics can confiscate for its own benefit. But faith is necessarily a demand for a certain political stance. Indeed a total cutting off of faith from politics is not possible except out of an *abstract* conception of Christian love and an individualistic and idealistic conception of the human subject. Under pretense of preserving the universalism of the Christian message people are ready to make concessions—as history bears out—to any kind of opportunism or any sort of compromise.

So the function of political theology is not only to thematize the political dimension and therefore the historical and eschatological dimension of Christianity. It ought to show in concrete terms how the Church is only faithful to its mission when it exercises a critical and liberating function in reference to human societies. That is why, while being co-extensive with all of theology, political theology will be most prominent in the area of the relations of the Church with the world. Concerning this Metz has also written a "theology of the world."[4]

Finally, political theology is striving to assume the permanent function of *fundamental theology* as a critical justification of the Christian faith in the eyes of unbelieving thinkers. It is in effect particularly qualified to demonstrate the credibility of Christianity for men who cannot accept a religion cut off from concrete human life and a God unconcerned with the becoming of the world. Its task will be twofold. On one hand it will exercise a critical function in respect to the tendency to reduce the Christian faith to the sphere of *private life* (privatization) in many contemporary theological currents. On the other hand it seeks to define new relations between religion and society, between eschatological faith and social practice.

A Program of "Deprivatizing"

The unwieldy word "deprivatizing" serves as a byword to designate Metz' theological program, just as the word "demythologizing" was used to designate Bultmann's approach. Rightly so, since "deprivatizing" as the first task of political theology ought to complete the legitimate task of "demythologizing." If not, "demythologizing" remains exposed to the danger of reducing God and salvation to being no more than correlatives of the private life of Christians.

Metz observes in the recent renewal of theology that the prominent categories are those of the intimate, the private, the interpersonal encounter. If they speak of love, it is always under its private and depoliticized form, as though it were exhausted in the "I-thou" encounter. These new forms of theology would then consecrate in modern times the divorce between religion and society, between faith and social practice.

This is especially true in Bultmann's *existential theology* which tends to concentrate the horizon of faith on the present moment of the personal decision of the believer to the detriment of the eschatological dimension of Christianity. It is a theology of *existence* which does not take enough account of man's socio-political conditioning. But Metz also moves away from the *transcendental theology* of his teacher Karl Rahner, who does have the merit of bringing out the existential significance of the statements of the faith for the man of today. However, this theology goes no further than an overly idealistic and individualistic conception of man which is reminiscent of reflective philosophy. Finally, Metz is determined to react against the various theologies of secularization (cf. Gogarten) which set apart the ineffable domain of the faith, while abandoning the world to its secularity, thereby maintaining Christianity imprisoned in the modern separation of the "private" from the "public."

In order to go beyond this "privatization" of theology which concentrates its attention on the present moment of faith, Metz, like Moltmann, starts with the eschatological announcement of the Kingdom and demonstrates its continuity with what is most characteristic of our modern culture—the orientation toward a future which is to be built practically. Starting with the *future* as the horizon for thought, we can interpret "the world as history, history as history of the end, faith as hope, and theology as eschatology." Our cultural and political situation, confronted with political and technical millenarianism as well as the hardening of established orders, urges us to demonstrate the "eschatological dimension" of all Christian theology. "Eschatology in a Christian theology ought to have a primary role, not just as a discipline beside other disciplines. . . . Eschatology must shape and determine *all* theological statements. . . . Only with the eschatological horizon of hope does the world appear as history. It is only such a conception which can establish on solid ground the permanent and fundamental significance of man and his free activity, and thereby allow for a theological understanding of the world" (p. 90).

The Church as the "Homeland of Freedom"

In order to understand the impact of the political theology of J.B. Metz, we must become aware of the dilemma in which contemporary Christianity is trapped: either a politicization which would question the separation of the spiritual and the temporal, or such a social and political neutrality that the faith would be increasingly relegated to the sphere of private life.

In fact, any theology which claims to be totally indifferent to its own socio-political conditioning runs the risk of playing the game of the "powers of this world" and of no longer respecting the critical and prophetic function of Christianity. Metz can speak of "political theology" without running the risk of making it an instrument for legitimizing the existing power structures, because for him "political" no longer means, as in former ecclesiastical thinking, the relative spheres of influence of Church and state, but rather the public democratic stage for the liberation of mankind.

The "political theology" of Metz makes note of the fact that the Church as an institution no longer has the monopoly on "publicity" for Christianity. It is up to each member of the people of God to take seriously the social and political implications of the Gospel. However, at the risk of shocking—this is one of the criticisms often directed against political theology—Metz demands the institutionalization of the critical freedom of the Christian. He rightly defines the Church as an *institution of social criticism*. The historical responsibility of Christianity toward the liberation of man is really too serious to be left up to the mere subjectivity of believers. While all too often in the past the Church has appeared as an "institution of repression," it must now see itself as an "institution of freedom," serving the cause of the liberation of man. The Church stands as the institutionalization of Christian freedom in the face of the "powers" of this world.

This critical role of the Church within societies is consistent with its nature: It should be in effect the practical and efficacious sign of eschatological hope. This means that it should denounce any status quo which would claim to be absolute. And the Church itself, as an institution, should submit itself to what Metz calls the "eschatological proviso" which implies the impossibility of absolutizing any historical accomplishment of society. "The Church herself as institution lives under the eschatological proviso. She is not for herself; she does not serve her own self-affirmation, but the historical affirmation of the salvation for all men. The hope she announces is not a hope for herself but for the kingdom of God. As institution, the Church truly lives on the proclamation of her own proviso. And she must realize this eschatological stipulation in that she establishes herself as the institution of critical liberty, in the face of society and its absolute and self-sufficient claims" (p. 116). We then see that the questioning role of the Church within societies is necessarily accompanied by a permanent reform within itself and a courageous overhauling of its dealings in the world.

The Church as the "homeland of freedom" should then constitute an historic force serving the cause of the liberation of man. Do we not then run the risk of falling back into a new sacralization of politics, no longer serving the interests of the "establishment," but now serving the ends of revolutionary ideologies? Metz' reply consists in invoking the "eschatological proviso" of the Church. In the name of the Gospel and its eschatological hope, the Church should exercise a *critical role* regarding the various forms of society and the various political ideologies which are always tempted to set themselves up as absolute.

However, it is not the place of the Church in our pluralistic society to propose a determined social order or a systematic social doctrine. Then theology would become a political ideology legitimizing a given form of Christian involvement.

The Challenging Force of Christian Hope

Nevertheless, we should not think that the political theology of Metz goes no further than pious generalities which might allow us to legitimize any kind of Christian attitude. It is precisely because it puts its hope beyond history that the Church protests any idolatrous closing in of society on itself. The critical judgment of the Church—even provisional—is therefore serving the concrete action of Christians confronted with urgent problems such as peace, social justice and development.

For example, it will be the role of the Church to defend the individual man against any social system which considers him as mere material for the building up of a totally rationalized technological future. The Church will also criticize all forms of totalitarianism, whether it is a case of the totalitarianism of money in capitalist societies or the totalitarianism of the state in socialist societies. Finally, the Church will do everything in its power to make the critical dynamism of Christian love manifest, which implies actualizing its properly social and political dimensions.

Metz strongly reminds us that Christian love demands a resolute criticism of pure violence. In general, he keeps his distance from any "theology of revolution," which to him seems too exposed to the "ideological" temptation of theology. However, he knows well that Christian love "can, in certain circumstances, demand actions of a revolutionary character" (p. 120). He even proposes a criterion for knowing when Christian love may lead to a revolutionary commitment: "If the status quo of a society contains as much injustice as would probably be caused by a revolutionary upheaval, then a revolution in favor of justice and freedom for the sake of 'the least of the brethren' cannot be forbidden in the name of that same love."

All these examples show us that there is a specific function for the Christian "utopia," even if it can never lead to the founding of a social order specifically Christian. I think that in the contemporary debate about the relation of the construction of the world to the coming of the Kingdom of God, the great merit of Metz' political theology is to invite us to go beyond false distinctions and comparisons.

Because the Church is witness to a hope beyond death it can work effectively for the social promotion of freedom in the restricted field of history. We must remove the paradox from the eschatological message of the Gospel. That is the error common to both absolute eschatologism and the various Christian messianisms. While the Church is radicalizing the involvement of Christians in the service of the world (it is a matter of anticipating here and now the accomplishment of the eschatological promise of peace, justice and freedom), it is at the same time relativizing it. We must not "sacralize" any status quo or social ideal as though we had no hope but in this world. Christian hope, as eschatological hope, is both *critical* toward the utopias of the future and *liberating* in respect to the heaviness of established orders.

Conclusion: The Future of Christianity

If I have chosen to restore the main intuitions and insights in the theological programs of Moltmann and Metz, it is because they are particularly significant of a whole orientation in contemporary Christianity and clearly manifest that the theology of today is striving to be the stage for the dialogue between the Church and the modern world. We could obviously criticize them for making too many concessions to certain fashionable ideas. In any case I think I have sufficiently shown that the accusation of "politicizing" theology which is leveled against "political theology" by superficial criticism will not hold up to examination. It would be more apt to criticize these two theological programs for not going beyond overly general views too abstract to really inspire any concrete application by Christians.

As I said above, it seems that these two theologies must above all be understood as *fundamental theologies* or critical reflections which attempt to insure the credibility of the Christian faith faced with modern intelligence. In order to do this, they start with a renewed reading of eschatology, to clearly bring out the social and political dimension of Christianity. It is on this ground that a critical discussion should be undertaken to check their scriptural basis and the manner in which they account for the entirety of the Christian message.

I would criticize Moltmann, for example, for being so obsessed with the future that he falls into a kind of *futurism*. His conception of historical *novelty* is so radical that he risks breaking the continuity of history and, by insisting on the "not yet," he undervalues the "already here" of Christian life as a theological and sacramental life. Moreover, his contrast of the theme of *epiphany* with that of the *promise* seems too absolute to account for all the aspects of the revelation of God in history. In this respect, we can wonder whether, like other contemporary theologians of *liberation*, he reads the New Testament too much in the light of the Old Testament, while the opposite must be also and perhaps primarily done.

As far as J.B. Metz is concerned, his conception of the Church as the *critical appeal* cannot but raise some questions. Is this a specifically Christian function and do we not run the risk of falling back into a new form of clericalism, as though the various struggles for justice needed the Church to be effective? The expression "political theology" itself may be irritating, because it could be suspected of being a compensation phenomenon in the face of the growing irrelevance of the Church in modern society.

No matter what can be said of these questions, I think Moltmann and Metz represent a new orientation in Christian theology. Their current reflection on salvation and the mission of the Church must definitely be taken into consideration. By showing that the *world*, and not only the individual or even the Church, is the aim of the saving plan of God, they invite us to not only place the earthly progress of the world side by side with the growth of the Kingdom, but to join them together.

The theological movement whose most original contribution I have tried to sum up is certainly a good indication of a majority trend within contemporary Christianity. Does it also prefigure the future of Christianity? I do not think so, to the extent that it reduces the Gospel too much to its *social usefulness* for the world. Is not political theology too obsessed with insuring the credibility of Christianity within a civilization greatly caught up with the utopias of the future? Moreover, this civilization is rapidly evolving under our very eyes. We are already at the dawn of a new cultural world which is no longer under the sign of Prometheus. Secretly the men of this world seem to be waiting for the *distinctive gratuity* of the Gospel to be manifested to them, that is a particular original message which they cannot hear elsewhere and which has something to say to man, even apart from any improvement of the world.

6. The Resurrection as the Center of Christian Theology

As strange as it may seem, the resurrection of Christ, which sums up all of Christianity, has still not been the object of any exhaustive reflection within dogmatic theology. The remark has often been made that the theology manuals devote little space to the resurrection compared to the long elaborations dealing with the divinity of Christ or with his redeeming mission. And even today, rare are the theologians who choose the resurrection of Christ as the organizing principle of Christology.[1]

This is not the place to explain why the most fundamental event in the history of salvation has only occupied a subordinate place in traditional dogmatics. We would have to retrace the history of Christianity and recall how, in the theology of the Latin Church, a moral and juridical conception of the redemption focusing on the merits of the passion and death of Christ has not allowed us to fully respect the salutary import of the resurrection.[2] The resurrection then becomes little more than the sign of God's acceptance of the sacrifice offered by his Son for the salvation of men. There is no doubt that the Paschal Mystery has always had a prominent place in Greek theology. But even there the resurrection is understood more as the crowning of the mystery of the divinization of man and of the world which has already been obtained through the incarnation.[3]

In any case it is certain that since the end of the nineteenth century the resurrection of Christ has become the favorite object of Christian apologetics. It was a matter of establishing the historicity of the resurrection in order to furnish a proof for the

divinity of Christ and thereby accredit his message and its legitimacy. And when apologetics had defended the historical character of the *miracle* of the resurrection, it seemed dogmatic theology had no more to say about the *mystery* of the resurrection.

Today, thanks to the biblical and liturgical renewal, the
Paschal Mystery is truly at the center of Christian piety. We
can no longer say as before that Good Friday eclipses Easter
morning as the main feast of Christendom. We can also rightly
acknowledge the availability of numerous exegetical works,
often noteworthy, on the resurrection. But even if it is difficult
to draw the line between exegesis and theology, we still cannot
say that the theology of the resurrection—at least on the Catholic side—is the focal point for theological reflection.

However, I would like to take into account the most significant trends in the current theological research on the resurrection of Christ. I shall begin by examining the source of the theological intelligibility of the resurrection. We shall see that the
renewal of the theology of the resurrection is linked to the
progress of hermeneutical reflection on the relationship between
event and *meaning* as well as to the re-reading of the resurrection of Christ as an eschatological event. The reinterpretation of
the resurrection in eschatological terms has proven very fertile
for dogmatics as a whole. The resurrection reveals to us the true
face of God and provides the starting point for a Christology; it
accounts for the dynamism of Christian existence and therefore
constitutes the foundation for a theology of hope and for the
mission of the Church. The two names which obviously domi-
nate this renewal of the theology of the resurrection are the
German Protestant theologians, Wolfhart Pannenberg and Jürgen Moltmann. Since a choice had to be made, you should not
be surprised if I make frequent reference to them.

The Resurrection as Event and as Language

If the theology of the resurrection has experienced for so
long a state of underdevelopment, it is probably because the attention of theologians has been too exclusively polarized by the

question of its historicity. Today, the new research invites us to no longer be content with historical investigation as the source of the theological intelligibility of the resurrection. The resurrection of Christ must be understood as an exemplary case of the encounter of reality and language.[4] The resurrection is inseparably both a real event situated in history and an event of the language of faith, a "word event" (*Wortgeschehen*), as the Germans call it. The testimonies of the Easter faith refer to real events, the apparitions. However, these events are not reported as *raw facts:* They are *interpreted* events. A rigorous analysis of the language of the resurrection shows us that it is to be properly understood not as an historical account but as a *confession of faith.*

It is obviously crucial to establish the *reality* of the resurrection event. If we refrain from designating the event as "historical" in the sense that it escapes any historical verification, that does not prevent it from being a real event which has left its mark on history—the apparitions, the empty tomb, the apostolic preaching. But by specifying that the event is only grasped in a confession of faith, we emphasize that it exists "fully and totally only if it is confessed, that is believed and proclaimed."[5] In other words, in becoming a "word event," the resurrection event takes on a new existence. At the source of the witness of the apostles there is both an "historical" experience and a faith experience. The meaning is certainly founded on a real and unexpected event, but it is an illusion to believe that the event can be dissociated from the new meaning it takes on in the faith account.[6]

Since Bultmann, it is certain that exegetical research has dealt less with the resurrection as an event which occurred to Jesus of Nazareth than with the *meaning* of the resurrection for us and as the object of apostolic preaching. But in Bultmann's case, you end up with an unacceptable break between fact and meaning. The resurrection becomes nothing more than the meaning of the cross for believers. "The Resurrection is nothing other than faith in the Cross as an event of salvation."

W. Marxen rejects this radical break between the event and the meaning, between history and faith.[7] For him, it is undeniable from the historical point of view that Jesus was *seen* after his death by the apostles. But the affirmation of the resurrection is only one *interpretation* among others of the immediate experience of the apostles. Insofar as it is not the objectification of a real event which happened to Jesus, this interpretation is legitimate. But more simply it means that the "Jesus affair" goes on, which is to say that Jesus continues to call forth a response from us today. Besides, the apostles themselves gave another interpretation to the apparition of the living Jesus when they understood it in terms of their "mission."

For Pannenberg, on the contrary, if Jesus is recognized as being alive, only one interpretation can account for this fact, namely that Jesus has truly risen or passed over into another life. He interprets the resurrection in terms of the apocalyptic expectation of the general resurrection of the dead. The resurrection of Christ is an *eschatological event*, because in it the ultimate reality of salvation has already come to pass. But this eschatological reality of salvation "takes root in the fact already accomplished in Jesus—and therefore historical—of the Resurrection of the dead."[8]

Despite differences in these works their most thought-provoking lesson is to make us more attentive to the inseparable link between historical experience and the language that interprets it. We always come in contact with the event through a certain kind of language. And, in the case of the resurrection, we note that the Easter faith cannot be reduced to any one of the kinds of language which express it. There can be no doubt that the language of the resurrection remains unique; it is the "language of reference" as X. Léon-Dufour puts it.[9] However, we must also be aware of the other kinds of language in the New Testament, such as those of *life* and *exaltation*, which rightly have the role of completing and complementing the vocabulary of the resurrection.

In other words, the event of the resurrection breaks through merely historical restrictions in that it is also a "word event." It is not just accomplished on the level of empirical history. According to the excellent formulation of H. Schleier, "by means of the apparitions, the Resurrection is fulfilled in the kerygma."[10] This brings us back to Bultmann's position in which the resurrection of Jesus is identified with his presence in the kerygma. This is as much as saying: "In virtue of the apparition of the risen and exalted Christ, the Resurrection of Jesus was expressed and transmitted in the witness of the disciples who saw him in that state. So, thanks to their word and witness, it penetrates into history and comes to encounter men."[11] Contrary to those who go no further than an historicizing conception of the resurrection, it may be affirmed that to the very extent that the resurrection is not reduced to the facticity of a bare fact and that it becomes the "statement" of a whole believing community it accedes to true historicity.

It is then an understatement or an overly obvious repetition to recall that we only attain the resurrection in the language of the Easter faith. We must underscore the *initiating* character of language in relation to the event. The theology of the resurrection is increasingly elusive to any exclusively apologetical controversy, because it no longer takes history with its empirical data as its only source of intelligibility. The proper source of the theological intelligibility of the mystery of the resurrection is to be found in the various kinds of language which express the Easter faith. Among these various kinds of language, the eschatological language seems to enjoy an especially prominent position. In the light of eschatological expectation we can understand the significance and the import of the resurrection. In any case we are going to see that the renewal of the theology of the resurrection and of Christology as a whole is closely connected with this discovery of the eschatological dimension.

The Resurrection of Jesus as Revelation of God

Most of the current work in Christology remains faithful to the classical Christology which came out of Chalcedon. This means they are essentially theologies of the incarnation which start "from above" with the divine filiation of Christ, to which have been added some insights from biblical theology on the titles of Christ, his messianic consciousness, his kenosis and his

Paschal Mystery. However Pannenberg, by resolutely starting "from below" with the historical life of Jesus, attempts to show that it is possible to respect the content of the dogma of Chalcedon on the divine filiation of Christ while abandoning the Christological method which came out of the controversy over the two natures, namely a descending Christology which begins with a theology of the incarnation. Instead of presupposing the divinity of Jesus, the task of dogmatics is to base the profession of faith "Jesus is Lord" on the history of Jesus, his message and the events of his life. This in no way means that such a Christology would be purely functional, leaving aside the question of the being of Christ.

On the contrary, the specific task of such a Christology would be to determine the relationship of Jesus to God and more precisely the God of Israel (since Jesus is historically situated). But his approach consists in discovering in Jesus the *revelation of God*, in showing how the resurrection is the foundation of his union with God. To put it another way, we must examine the union of this unique man Jesus with the God of Israel instead of proceeding with an *a priori* reflection on the general possibility of the union of God and man in Jesus. In this perspective the very word "God" can only be understood in terms of the particularity of the history of Jesus of Nazareth. The true question is not "Can we know God in Jesus Christ?" but rather "Who is the God that we know in Jesus Christ?"

But Pannenberg does not only move away from classical Christologies which start "from above," but also from contemporary Christologies which start "from below," attempting to base the union of Jesus with God not on his resurrection but on the claim to divine omnipotence contained in his preaching and his action.[12] Pannenberg on the contrary thinks that "the union of Jesus with God does not have its basis in the claim implied in His pre-paschal actions, but only in his Resurrection from the dead."[13]

Jesus' claim to divine omnipotence can only be understood in the context of the apocalyptic traditions of Israel, which express hope in the final revelation of God at the end of time and the hope in the resurrection of the dead coinciding with that revelation. Jesus announces the imminence of the Kingdom. To decide for or against Jesus is to already decide one's eternal salvation. However, this extravagant claim of Jesus' seems to have been checked by his death on the cross. Even more it appears as a sacrilege, since he is condemned on account of his claim to divine omnipotence. So only the experience of the apostles after the death of Jesus enables them to attest to the legitimacy of Jesus' claim.

It is then the resurrection which is the basis for Jesus' claim to omnipotence and which makes manifest his union with God. Thanks to the resurrection, the whole life of Jesus before Easter becomes the ultimate revelation of God for which Israel had been waiting. A being's meaning can only be found in its ultimate end. The life of Jesus takes on its meaning as revelation of God only in the resurrection. By speaking of retroactive significance of the resurrection for the whole life of the pre-Paschal Jesus, the theology of the resurrection really takes seriously the fact that, for the New Testament, the resurrection is the starting point for faith in Christ the Lord.

More must be said, however. Because the resurrection is a proleptic event, which is to say the anticipation of the end of history, it is already the definitive revelation of God. According to the conception of revelation proper to Pannenberg, events as acts of God are what indirectly reveal to us something about God. And since even a particular can only provide a partial revelation of God, the full self-revelation of God is only possible when the whole of history is regarded as revelation. The full revelation of God will then coincide with the completion of history. Moreover, history reveals God because the end of history is *anticipated* in the resurrection of Christ.

"Only at the end of all history can God appear in his divinity, that is, as He who has made everything and who has power over all things. Because, in the Resurrection, the end of all things which for us is still to come has for Jesus already taken place, it is possible to say that the definitive is already present in him and therefore that God and His glory are manifested in Jesus in an unsurpassable manner. Only because the end of the world is already present in the Resurrection of Jesus does God reveal Himself in him."[14]

Therefore the revelation of God and the revelation of the

meaning of history cannot be separated. It remains for us to show how the resurrection of Christ is the key to universal history.

The Resurrection and the Meaning of History

Today Western thought has been becoming increasingly critical of rational reconstruction of history in the Hegelian sense. Any philosophy of history which would claim to read an overall meaning into history seems doomed to failure. Pannenberg does not hesitate, however, to elaborate a theology of history from the Hegelian idea of history considered as a whole which only takes on its full meaning at its completion. He therefore chooses universal history as the hermeneutical principle for his theology of history. The proper area for theology is history itself, but considered in eschatological terms.

Pannenberg rejects any Manichaean distinction between history of salvation and secular history. There is only one history and that is history taken as a whole which is revelation of God. He therefore moves away from any conception of "salvation history" which, by taking refuge in a "supra-history" or supernatural history, cuts the link between revelation and history. On the other hand he objects to the theologies of the word (like Bultmann's), which by concentrating on the historicity of man no longer show how God is the subject of all history.

What the historian or the philosopher can only intimate, namely the idea of a meaning to history or a rationality immanent to history, the theologian affirms with certainty. If history is a totality opened on to a completion and if it is something other than a succession of merely contingent events, it is because it has a transcendent foundation, God. But that is saying too little. A unity of history can only be conceived in terms of its end. For us this end remains an unforeseeable future. But the theologian knows that this end has been anticipated in the eschatological event of the resurrection of Christ. In the resurrection as the "prolepsis" of the end of history, we have the key to universal history and can discover the meaning of any particular period.

However, if it is true that a particular event can only manifest its whole meaning at the end of history, this is also true of the Jesus Christ event itself. "We do not yet know in any definitive way what really happened in the ministry and destiny of Jesus."[15] Pannenberg therefore rejects the Hegelian idea of an *absolute knowledge* and maintains the limited and temporary character of our historical knowledge. As long as history remains incomplete, we cannot lay claim to any definitive knowledge, even if its meaning is anticipated in Christ. History remains open to an unforeseeable future. It does repeat former events but not without bringing in something new. God is the subject of history, but God's presence in history must be thought of as the presence of the future in the present, as what enables the present to be open and not closed in on itself, and certainly not as the presence of eternity in time.

With the resurrection of Christ, the last times have been inaugurated, the eschatological reality of salvation has already come to pass and every man who decides for Jesus already belongs to the new creation. However the dialectic of the "already" and the "not yet" must not be ignored or forgotten. History is still waiting in expectation for the full and definitive accomplishment of the promises contained in the resurrection of Christ. The Christian lives in the hope of that ultimate fulfillment of history which will be the Kingdom announced by Jesus, a community of justice, peace and love.

Considered in itself, history retains its ambiguity and its obscurity: It is more a stage for contradiction and failure. And left to itself, history is incapable of accomplishing its own fulfillment. But the victory over the defeat of the cross proclaimed in the resurrection is the promise that God will take up all human history to make it succeed. The Christian, as a witness to the resurrection, therefore also bears witness to the meaning of history and its stretching toward an ultimate fulfillment. And bearing witness implies even further the actualizing of the Kingdom of God among men, manifesting the active power of love.

This is the kind of vision of history which is inspired by a theology of the resurrection. We can only regret that Pannenberg is not very explicit about the meaning of history after the resurrection of Christ and about the relation of present history to the eschatological completion of that history in the second coming of Christ.

The Theology of the Resurrection
as a Theology of Hope

J. Moltmann's theology of hope is also a theology of the resurrection interpreted from the notion of eschatological expectation. Like Pannenberg, he seeks to react against the existential theology of Bultmann which is locked up in the interiority of faith, and to demonstrate the radical link between eschatology and history. Indeed, we must avoid any distinction that would confine the faith to the private sphere and leave the world to its own impulses and to its secularity. While subscribing to the same trend of thought as Pannenberg, Moltmann criticizes him for being content to propose just another *interpretation* of universal history. He himself attempts to demonstrate the historical efficacy of Christianity for the *transformation* of history and of man in his social and political dimensions. We have already quoted the sentence which best sums up his whole theological approach: "The theologian is therefore not satisfied with supplying a different interpretation of the world, history and the human condition; for him it is a matter of *transforming* them in expectation of a divine transformation." That is why his theology of hope, which chooses the resurrection as its focal point, is also a *political theology* and a theology of the *mission* of the Church.

The only way to properly respect the eschatological dimension of Christianity without placing history in brackets is to rediscover the original conception of history proper to the biblical tradition. The real point of difference between the Greek conception and the Jewish conception of history is the difference between *epiphany* and *promise*. By taking as the key to the history of Israel the "promise-fulfillment" dialectic, Moltmann invites us to re-think the relationship between God and history (cf. *supra*, p. 82).

The whole intent of Moltmann's work is to interpret the

resurrection of Christ in terms of the Jewish theology of the promise and thereby found a *theology of hope* which is at the same time a *political theology.* As we have seen in the preceding chapter, it is not sufficient to understand the resurrection of Christ as the fulfillment of the promise which puts an end to history. It must be shown how the resurrection of Christ does not exhaust the promise of God but refers us to the future. This is why the promise must not be understood in reference to an epiphanic God, to the God who is, but rather to the God who is coming and whose promise is never exhausted by his historical accomplishments. Even if the resurrection of Christ is already the anticipated fulfillment of God's promise, it is not yet the final fulfillment.

This reinterpretation of the resurrection of Christ in the context of the promise renews the theology of hope. It could be said that Christian hope is an ontological reality to the extent that it is based on that anticipation of the future as the mode of being most proper to God, which is fulfilled and revealed in the resurrection of Christ. It specifies human existence as Christian existence and is inseparable from faith. It must even be said that it exercises a kind of primacy in regard to faith, since it is like the *creative power* of faith in that it makes a life of faith possible here below. "So, in the Christian life, faith has the priority but hope has the primacy. Without the knowledge of Christ by faith, hope becomes a utopia launching out into empty space. But without hope, faith withers away, becoming a 'weak faith' and finally a dead faith. By faith man arrives on the path to true life, but only hope keeps him on that path. . . . To believe means to infringe through anticipating hope on the restrictions that the Resurrection of the Crucified Lord has broken through. If we reflect on it, this faith can have nothing in common with a flight from the world or any kind of resignation or escapism. In this hope, the soul does not leave this valley of tears to go soaring through an imaginary heaven of the blessed, it does not separate itself from the earth. . . . This hope discerns in the Resurrection of Christ not the eternity of heaven, but the future of this very earth on which his Cross is raised."[17]

Christian hope, having as its object the resurrection of

Christ and the totality of the new creation, becomes in the heart of reality a power of contradiction and a "creative transformation" of reality. We could call Christian hope anti-fatalistic, since he who hopes never resigns himself to the necessities of this world, or to the inevitability of death or to the irreversibility of evil. "The Resurrection of Christ is not only for him a consolation in a life of trial condemned to die, but also the contradiction brought by God to suffering and death, to humiliation and injury, to the wickedness of the wicked. For hope, Christ is not only a consolation *in* suffering, but also the protest of the promise of God *against* suffering."[18]

In this perspective, Christian hope does not only bear on "something beyond" history. Thanks to hope the history of the "future of God" is already present in the heart of the present. Hope denies that the real is only what it is now—hope opens it to the future. Hope denies that history is no more than the same thing over and over again—hope opens it to the new.

Moltmann reverses the manner in which we usually connect human expectation and the promise of God. Instead of making Christian hope one of the modalities of human hope in general, the various human hopes appear as specifications of Christian hope. Saint Augustine's *cor inquietum*, far from being just a general human condition, as presupposed by the Christian reply which comes to put it to rest, is rather the consequence of the *promissio inquieta* contained in Christian revelation. The resurrection of Christ, as memory of the promise of God which came into our history, becomes like a "thorn in the flesh" planted into every present to open it to the future. "In this sense, the revelation of the Risen Lord does not become 'historic' (in the strict sense of *geschichtlich*) as a result of the fact that history continues its aimless flow; it stands on the contrary, as a sort of *primum movens* at the head of the historical process. The reality of man and of his world becomes through it 'historic,' and the hope set on this revelation makes all reality inadequate, and as such transient and surpassable. This is the *promissio inquieta* which in fact gives birth to the Augustinian *cor inquietum*."[19]

If we take seriously the transforming energy of the resurrection of Christ at work in history, we must not only speak of a theology of hope but of *political theology.* Christian hope indeed has a revolutionary character. Revolution, in Moltmann's sense, is only possible where the future harbors in it a radical possibility of transformation. And the future, as the object of Christian hope, ought to be understood as "the freedom for the new" which implies the transformation of all historical reality in the light of the *eschaton.* Thus, revolution in its most authentic sense is none other than the transformation of reality on the basis of an eschatological horizon. The revolutionary dimension of Christian hope does not lead the Church to espouse any type of combat whatsoever, but only those struggles which are like anticipations of a greater revolution, that of the *new creation,* announced in the words of Revelation: "Behold I make all things new" (Rev. 21:5).

The revolutionary dynamic of Christian hope which is based on the resurrection of Christ as anticipation of the future promised by God can never be satisfied with a limited objective. It denounces any idolatry of an historical form of society at the same time it subjects to a demanding critique any utopia concerning the future of humanity. However, it assumes and radicalizes all legitimate human hopes which inspire an effective struggle for the historical transformation of the human condition in the direction of greater justice and the humanization of man.

As I have already said above (cf. *supra*, pp. 87ff.), the theology of hope, renewed in the light of the mystery of the resurrection, necessarily opens out to a theology of the mission of the Church. Its mission essentially consists in actualizing the possibilities for the future which are contained in the event of the resurrection of Christ. At a time when the Church is more and more sensitive to the fact that it cannot dissociate its preaching of the Kingdom from its historical responsibilities to the world, unquestionably the most positive lesson of Moltmann's *theology of hope* is to invite us to a re-reading of the New Testament. Then we discover that the expectation of the Kingdom which is not of this world, as Christ founded it in the blood of his cross, does not nullify the humble promises of the Old Testament concerning a reconciliation of humanity within history itself.

However, to pass a critical judgment on the reinterpretation of Christian eschatology proposed by Moltmann would need a new chapter. My only aim here was to suggest how, in the line of authors like Pannenberg and Moltmann, we are experiencing today a very promising renewal of the theology of the resurrection. It is from the eschatological horizon that the resurrection of Christ must be *theologically* reinterpreted. We are not only justly crediting the most decisive contribution of biblical theology; it is now possible to show how the mystery of the resurrection of Christ constitutes the most fertile link of intelligibility for properly posing some very current questions, such as the relation of theological faith to Christian practice, of eschatological expectation of the Kingdom to the earthly progress of the world.

Theology, as a human and therefore historical science of the faith, is a task which is ever new. The hour has come, it seems, for Christian theology to seek to *get beyond* what still opposes a theology of *conversion* to a theology of *history*. And I believe that the unfailing mediation of the mystery of the resurrection of Christ will enable this progress to be a real fulfillment of what is irreducible in each of these theologies.

Footnotes

CHAPTER 1

1. From a long list of studies, I specifically refer to the following: A. Gaboardi, "Teologia fondamentale. Il metodo apologetico," in *Problemi e Orientamenti di teologia dommatica* I (Milan, 1957), pp. 57-92; A. Lang, *Fundamentaltheologie. Die Sendung Christi* (Munich, ³1962), pp. 8-40; G. Söhngen, "Fundamentaltheologie," in *Lex Theol. u. Kirche* (4th ed.), pp. 452-59; A. Kolping, *Fundamentaltheologie* I (Münster, 1968), pp. 21-87; N. Dunas, "Les problèmes et le statut de l'Apologétique," in *Rev. Sc. Phil. et Théol.* 43 (1959), pp. 643-80; H. Bouillard, *Logique de la foi* (Paris, 1964), pp. 15-44.

2. *Dictionnaire de la foi Chrétienne* I (Paris, 1968), col. 769.

3. Y. Congar, *La foi et la théologie* (Paris, 1962), p. 183.

4. H. Bouillard suggests that we call the study of the *loci theologici* the "prolegomena to dogmatic theology" and that we reserve the expression "fundamental theology" for what is usually called "apologetics"; see his article "Human Experience as the Starting Point of Fundamental Theology," in *Concilium* 6 (1965), p. 80.

5. Söhngen stresses this third meaning in his article referred to in footnote 1. See also the observations of J.P. Torrel, who compares this critical function of fundamental theology with the function of the treatise on criticism in philosophy, in "Chronique de théologie fondamentale," in *Rev. Thom.* 64 (1964), pp. 101-02.

6. For an historical outline, see A. Kolping, *op. cit.*, pp. 35-70.

7. Cf. J.H. Walgrave, *Parole de Dieu et existence* (Paris, 1967), pp. 198-201, and also his article in this volume.

8. This threefold division appears already in P. Charron, *Des trois vérités* (1514), and in the Protestant thinker H. Grotius, *De veritate religionis christianae* (1627).

9. I refer to the article "Apologétique" in *Dictionnaire d'Apologétique* where P. Le Bachelet defines apologetics as "the science whose object is to prove the fact of divine revelation considered as the foundation of the true religion or the science of the credibility of the Christian and Catholic religion" (I, col. 225). And the encyclical *Humani generis* declares that the outward signs dispensed by God "allow-natural reason, even by itself, to prove the origin of the Christian religion with certainty."

10. Cf. H. de Lubac, "Commentaire du préambule et du chapitre I," in *La Révélation divine* I (Paris, 1968), p. 283, who quotes P. Dejaifve, *Nouv. Rev. Théol.* (1966), p. 124.

11. This expression is used by H. Fries, "Die Offenbarung," in *Mysterium Salutis* I (Einsiedeln, 1965), p. 159.

12. N. Dunas, "Les problèmes et le statut de l'apologétique," in *Rev. sc. phil. théol.* 43 (1959), p. 679. Even if it does not convey the whole program of a fundamental theology, many authors would accept the following definition: "A critical theology of the Word of God in its being and its manifestations, in its sources and its means of expression" (*ibid.*, p. 680).

13. See L. Bakker, "What Is Man's Place in Divine Revelation?" in *Concilium*, 21 (1967), p. 31.

14. J.M. Walgrave, *op. cit.*, 202.

15. While traditional apologetics admitted that the judgment of credibility preceded the act of faith and made it reasonable, Rousselot thought that this judgment did not precede but was implied in the act of faith: the light of faith lets us see that credibility. Rousselot's view was developed by Tiberghien and de Masure.

16. The expression "the *human* credibility of Christianity" appears in P.A. Liege, "Bulletin d'Apologétique," in *Rev. sc. phil. théol.* 33 (1949), p. 67.

17. H. Bouillard, "Human Experience as the Starting Point of Fundamental Theology," in *Concilium* 6 (1965), pp. 79f. His plan for apologetics must be understood in this perspective. Taking up Blondel's "immanent" approach, he tries to show that our relation to the Absolute is and must be with reference to the dynamism of our will, in order to bring out the fact that Christianity is the historical determination of this relation.

18. P. Ricoeur, "Le langage de la foi," in *Bulletin du Centre protestant d'Etudes* 16 (June, 1964), p. 31.

19. K. Rahner, "Theology and Anthropology," in *The Word in History* (New York, 1968).

20. *Ibid.*

21. *Ibid.*

22. This is the only point on which I disagree with L. Malevez in his finely balanced article on the twofold tendency in contemporary theology, "Présence de la théologie à Dieu et à l'homme," in *Nouv. Rev. Théol.* 90 (1968), p. 799.

23. K. Rahner, *op. cit.* See also his "Ueber die theoretische Ausbildung künftiger priester heute," in *Schriften zur Theologie* VI (Einsiedeln, 1965), p. 154.

24. On Heidegger's hermeneutical phenomenology, based on the hermeneutics of factual reality, see O. Pöggeler, *Der Denkweg Martin Heideggers* (Pfullingen, 1963), pp. 70f.

25. "Revelation presupposes man's quest for himself as the condi-

tion for the meaning of his self. That is why faith, the confession of faith and dogma can only have meaning *in* man's self-understanding. . . . Man's self-understanding is therefore an internal dimension of revelation itself": E. Schillebeeckx, "The Understanding of Faith and Self-Interpretation," in *The Word in History* (New York, 1968).

26. K. Rahner, "Ueber die theoretische Ausbildung künftiger Priester heute," in *Schriften zur Theologie VI* (Einsiedeln, 1965), p. 152.

27. *Ibid.*

28. H. Urs von Balthasar, *Herrlichkeit* I (Einsiedeln, 1961), p. 142, quoted by L. Malevez, *art. cit.*, p. 794.

29. *Ibid.*

30. *Ibid.*, p. 446.

31. Quoted by H. Ott, "Was ist systematische Theologie?" in *Der spätere Heidegger und die Theologie* (Zurich, 1964), p. 132.

32. L. Malevez, *art. cit.*, 797.

33. See esp. J. Moltmann, *Theologie der Hoffnung* (Munich, 1965) and J.B. Metz, "L'Eglise et le monde," in *Théologie d'aujourd'hui et de demain* (Paris, 1967), pp. 139-54 and "The Church's Social Function in the Light of a 'Political Theology,' " in *Concilium* 36 (1968), pp. 2-18.

34. J. B. Metz, "L'Eglise et le monde," *op. cit.*, 140.

35. *Ibid.*, pp. 147-48.

36. J.B. Metz, "The Church's Social Function in the Light of a 'Political Theology,' " *op. cit.*, p. 6.

37. E. Schillebeeckx, "La théologie du renouveau parle de Dieu," in *La théologie du renouveau* I (Montreal/Paris, 1968), p. 102.

CHAPTER 2

1. You may refer to my 1968 article about the "crisis in theology" ("La crise de la théologie") in *Avenir de la théologie*, Paris, 1968, pp. 57-66.

2. See Ladriere's basic study "La théologie et le langage de l'interprétation." *Revue théologique de Louvain*, I (1970), pp. 241-267.

3. Cf. G. Martelet, "Remarques sur l'unité anthropologique des sciences et de la théologie" in *Sciences et Théologie* (Recherche et Débats, 67), Paris, 1969, pp. 29-34.

4. J.P. Jossua's contribution to the theology congress in Brussels is a good example of this trend.

5. Refer to M. De Certeau's provocative study, "L'articulation du 'dire' et du 'faire' la contestation universitaire indice d'une tache théologique." *Et. théol. et rel.* 45 (1970), pp. 25-40.

6. Karl Rahner, "La réflexion théologique en philosophie" in

Ecrits théologiques 11, *Axes théologiques pour demain*, Paris, 1970, p. 61.

7. In regard to this crisis of the objectivity of God, refer to my study, "Le probléme théologique de l'objectivité de Dieu" in *Procès de l'objectivité de Dieu*, Paris, 1969, pp. 241-276.

8. A. Dumas has attempted to sketch at the time of D. Bonhoeffer's theological work, what such a theology of reality could be: cf. *Une théologie de la réalité Dietrich Bonhoeffer*, Labor et Fides, 1968.

9. G. Granel, "Sur la situation de l'incroyance," *Esprit* (janvier 1971), pp. 13-14.

10. We take our inspiration here from M. Xhauffaire who distinguished, in reaction to Feuerbach's works, the "positivist" theologies, the theology of mediation and the theologies of dialogue: cf. *Feuerbach et la théologie de la sécularisation*, Paris, 1970, pp. 307-339.

11. Cf. W. Pannenberg, *Grundzüge der Christologie*, Gütersloh, 1964; English translation, *Jesus, God and Man*, Philadelphia, 1968.

12. Cf. G. Lafont, *Peut-on connaitre Dieu en Jésus Christ?* Paris, 1969. You may read the judicious critical remarks of B.D. Rey on this work in his note "Théologie trinitaire et révélation biblique," *Rev. sc. phil. théol.* 54 (1970), pp. 636-653.

13. I have attempted to clarify the meaning of this transition in my study: "La théologie de l'histoire comme problème herméneutique" in *Herméneutique et Eschatologie* (Actes du Colloque Romain, Jan. 1971), pp. 45-59. Cf. *infra*, Chapter 4, pp. 66ff.

14. See in particular Pannenberg, "Hermeneutik und Universalgeschichte" in *Grundfragen systematisher Theologie*, Göttingen, 1967, pp. 99-122. English translation: "Hermeneutics and Universal History" in *Basic Questions in Theology*, Philadelphia, pp. 97-120.

15. Cf. J. Moltmann, *Theologie der Hoffnung*, Munich, 1964; English translation: *Theology of Hope*, Harper & Row, New York 1967.

16. R. Bultmann, *Jésus, Mythologie et démythologisation*, French translation, Le Seuil, 1968, preface by Paul Ricoeur, pp. 9-28. The English translation of this work of Bultmann's is *Jesus and the Word*, Herder & Herder, New York, 1969.

17. Cf. *supra*, pp. 46ff., what I have already said about the consequences of this hermeneutical orientation of theology concerning the relations between *fundamental* theology and *dogmatic* theology.

18. Cf. W. Kasper, *Dogme et Evangile*, Paris, 1967, pp. 130-133; translation of the original German *Dogma unter dem Wort Gottes*, Mainz 1965.

19. W. Kasper has briefly traced the history of this divorce in his study: *Renouveau de la méthode théologique*, Paris 1968.

CHAPTER 3

1. L. Wittgenstein, *Tractatus Logico-Philosophicus*, new translation by D.F. Pears and B.F. McGuinness (London and New York, 1961) 4003.

2. Cf. Landon Gilkey, *Naming the Whirlwind: The Renewal of God-Language* (New York, 1969), pp. 13-25.

3. The expression "semantic atheism" is used by D. Antiseri in *Foi sans métaphysique ni théologie* (Paris, 1970), p. 32.

4. Cf. J. Ladrière, "Théologie et langage de l'intérpretation," *Rev. théol. de Louvain* I (1970), p. 258.

5. O. Pöggeler, *La Pensée de Martin Heidegger* (Paris, 1967), p. 384 (*Der Denkweg Martin Heideggers:* Pfüllingen, 1963).

6. I have explained my ideas on this new age in theology at greater length in my study "L'objectivité propre au Dieu révélé," in *L'analyse du langage théologique. Le nom de Dieu* (Paris, 1969), pp. 403-21.

7. Cf. Cl. Geffré, "Théologie naturelle et révélation dans la connaissance du Dieu un," in *L'existence de Dieu*, Cahiers de l'actualité religieuse 16 (Paris, 1963), pp. 297-317, and B. Montagnes, "Le Dieu de la philosophie et le Dieu de la foi," in *Procès de l'objectivité de Dieu* (Paris, 1969), pp. 215-31.

8. B. Welte, "La métaphysique de S. Thomas d'Aquin et la pensée de l'histoire de l'etre chez Heidegger," *Revue des sciences philosophiques et théologiques* 50 (1965), p. 612.

9. Cf. A. Dumas, "La critique de l'objectivité de Dieu dans la théologie protestante," in *Procès de l'objectivité de Dieu, op. cit.*, pp. 147-68.

10. See W. Schulz's *Der Gott der neuzeitlichen Metaphysik* (Pfüllingen, 1967). Schulz has shown brilliantly how God in the modern age has become the medium and the condition of possibility for man's spiritual fulfillment.

11. Cf. K. Löwith, *From Hegel to Nietzsche* (London, 1969), Chapter 5 (*Von Hegel zu Nietzsche*, Zürich, 1941).

12. I have taken these expressions from Paul Ricoeur's preface to the French translation of Bultmann's *Jesus* (Paris, 1968, p. 28).

13. M. Heidegger, "Quelques indications sur des points de vue principaux du colloque théologique consacré au 'Problème d'une pensée et d'un langage non-objectivants dans la théologie d'aujourd'hui'," unpublished text of 1964 in *Archives de Philosophie* 32 (1969), p. 413.

14. On the movement of thought in non-metaphysical theology, see my "L'objectivité propre au Dieu révélé," *art. cit.*, pp. 413ff.

CHAPTER 4

1. "Heidelberg circle" has been used to designate this new theological current. The result of this work in common was the publication in 1961 of the first edition of *Offenbarung als Geschichte*, Göttingen. *Revelation as History*, New York, 1968.

2. Cf. "Die Krise des Chriftprinzips," in *Grundfragen systematischer Theologie*, Göttingen 1967, pp. 16-17; English translation: "Crisis of the Scripture Principle" in *Basic Questions in Theology*, Fortress, Philadelphia 1968, pp. 8-9.

3. This keynote often recurs in Pannenberg and corresponds to the word *Entmythologisierung* in Bultmann's program. See for example Pannenberg's article in the collective work *Theologie als Geschichte. Neuland in der Theologie.*, vol. 3, Zurich 1967, p. 264. You will see in this same volume an excellent contribution by J.M. Robinson, "Offenbarung als Wort und Geschichte," which historically situates Pannenberg's theology and evaluates the criticism directed toward him.

4. "Dogmatische Eerwägungen zur Auferstehung Jesu," *Kerygma und Dogma* 14 (1968), p. 108, quoted by I. Berten, *Histoire, révélation et foi, Dialogue avec Wolfhart Pannenberg*, Brussels 1969, p. 46. We will refer several times to this excellent introduction to Pannenberg's difficult thought.

5. "Redemptive Event and History" in *Basic Questions.* . . .

6. See my study "Kérygme et histoire chez Rudolf Bultmann" in *Revue des Sciences philosophiques et théologiques* 49 (1965), pp. 609-639.

7. Cf. "Heilsgeschehen und Geschichte," *ibid.* (Salvation Event and History) ". . . flüchtete die heilsgeschichtliche Theologie in der vermeintlich vor der historisch-kritischen Flut sicheren Hafen einer Ubergeschichte, oder, mit Barth, einer Urgeschichte. Aus dem gleichen Grund zog sich die Existenztheologie zurück vom sinn- und heillosen 'objektiven' Geschehensablauf auf die Erfahrung der Beceutsamkeit der Geischichte in der 'Geschichtlichkeit' des einzelnen."

8. M. Seil, "Théologie de l'existence et théologie de l'histoire devant la philosophie du langage et la théologie de la parole," in *Archives de philosophie* 33 (1970), p. 252. Article already appearing in the *Neue Zeitschrift für systematische Theologie und Religionsphilosophie* 7 (1965), I.

9. "Geschichte ist der umfassendste Horizont christlicher Theologie." This is the first sentence of "Heilsgeschehen und Geschichte." ("Redemptive Event and History" in *Basic Questions* . . . ,p. 15).

10. We see the first theological use of this distinction in Martin Kahler's article *The So-Called Historical Jesus and the Historic Biblical Christ*, Phila., 1964; for the use of this distinction in Bultmann, see G, Greshake, *Historie und Geschichte in der Theologie Rudolf Bult-*

mann, Essen, 1963; see also Geffré, *art. cit.*, pp. 615 ff.

11. "Hermeneutik und Universalgeschichte" in *Grundfragen* . . . , p. 99 (English edition *Basic Questions* . . . , p. 108).

12. *Grundfragen* . . . , p. 101; *Basic Questions* . . . , p. 110. "Er muss die Aussagen über Gott als blossen *Ausdruck* eines zugrunde liegenden Existenzverständnis auflassen."

13. *Basic Questions* . . . , pp. 115-116.

14. *Ibid.*, p. 123.

15. *Ibid.*

16. *Ibid.*, pp. 129-130.

17. I. Berten, *op. cit.*, p. 27.

18. "Gadamer hat damit den Sachverhalt formuliert, der in der Tat alles heute mögliche Denken von Hegel trennt und eine einfach Wiederholung der Systematik Hegels unmöglich macht; Die Endlichkeit als Standpunkt des Denkens und Offenheit der Zukunft" (*Grundfragen* . . . , p. 110; *Basic Questions* . . . , pp. 121-122).

19. "Redemptive Event and History" in *Basic Questions* . . . , p. 78. Pannenberg again explains his position and what separates him from Cullmann's conception in his epilogue to *Theologie als Geschichte*, pp. 316-317.

20. This is Pannenberg's first thesis on revelation: "Die Selbstoffenbarung Gottes hat sich nach den Biblischen Zeugnissen nicht direkt, etwa in der Weise einer Theophanie, sondern indirekt, durch Gottes Geschichtstaten, vollzogen" (cf. "Dogmatische Thesen zur Lehre von der Offenbarung" in *Offenbarung als Geschichte*, p. 91).

21. *Theologie als Geschichte*, p. 32.

22. Uber historische und theologische Hermeneutik" ("On Historical and Theological Hermeneutic" in *Basic Questions* . . . , p. 180).

23. I. Berten, *op. cit.*, p. 45.

24. "Einsicht und Glaube" in *Grundfragen* . . . , p. 230 (quoted by I. Berten on p. 51 note 72).

25. See Pannenberg's study "Glaube und Vernunft" in *Grundfragen* . . . , pp. 237-251.

26. Paul Ricoeur, in his preface to the French translation of the *Jésus* of Bultmann observes that the author did not go far enough in his criticism of the language of faith as soon as it ceases to be "objectivizing." This is particularly true of the expressions "Word of God," and "act of God." "What is not not thought out enough in Bultmann is the properly non-mythological kernel of Biblical and theological statements, and therefore also by contrast, the mythological statements themselves." (*Jésus: Mythologie et démythologisation*, Paris, 1968, p. 22)

27. J. Moltmann, *Theology of Hope*, Harper & Row, New York 1967, p. 84.

28. *Op. cit.*, p. 77; see also pp. 272-275.

29. *Op. cit.*, p. 264.
30. Cf. *Theologie als Geschichte*, pp. 320-321.
31. Moltmann, *op. cit.*, p. 86.
32. J. Moltmann, "L'espérance sans foi. Réflexion sur l'humanisme eschatologique sans Dieu," in *Concilium* 16 (1966), p. 48.

CHAPTER 5

1. J. Moltmann, *Theology of Hope*, New York 1967. This reading may be rounded out by Moltmann's two synthetical conferences, "La religion de l'espérance" and "Introduction à la theologie de l'espérance" in *Etudes théologiques et religieuses* 46 (1971), pp. 385-398, 399-414.
2. J.B. Metz, *Theology of the World*, Herder & Herder, New York 1969. Other writings by J.B. Metz: "Théologie politique et liberté critico-sociale," *Concilium* 36 (1968), pp. 9-25 and "La présence de l'Eglise dans la société," Concilium 60 Supp. (1970), pp. 91-101.
3. P. Ricoeur, "La liberté selon l'espérance," in *Le conflit des interprétations*, Seuil, 1969, p. 396.
4. *Theology of the World*, J.B. Metz, to which the quotations in this section refer.

CHAPTER 6

1. To cite a recent example, C. Ducoqu's *Christologie* in the first volume deals with the titles of Christ and puts the study of the Paschal Mystery into the second volume. We have to say the same for G. Lafont's *Peut-on connaitre Dieu en Jésus Christ?* which is essentially a theology of the incarnation.
2. Karl Rahner thereby explains the main reason for the fading of the theology of the resurrection in "Questions dogmatiques se rapportant à la dévotion pascale" in *Ecrits théologiques*, v. i, Paris-Bruges, 1967, pp. 143-159.
3. For this delicate point on the history of doctrines, refer to the work of J.P. Jossua, *Le salut: incarnation ou mystère pascal*, Paris, 1968.
4. In French the two most noteworthy exegetical works which reinterpret the resurrection of Christ in this perspective are those of X. Léon-Dufour, *Résurrection de Jésus et Message pascal*, Paris 1971 and of J. Delorme in *Le langage de la foi dans l'Ecriture et dans le monde actuel*, "La Résurrection de Jésus dans le langage du Nouveau Testament," Paris 1971, pp. 101-182.
5. A. Gesche, "La Résurrection de Jésus dans la théologie dogmatique," Revue théologique de Louvain, 1971, 2, p. 295.

6. For a more exhaustive reflection on the relationship between historical experience and language in the faith account, see my study "Le témoignage comme expérience et comme langage" in *Le témoignage*, Colloque romain 5-11 January 1972, edited by E. Castell, Paris 1972, pp. 291-307.

7. Cf. W. Marxen, *The Resurrection of Jesus of Nazareth*, Philadelphia 1970. A critical exposition of Marxen's theology of the resurrection can be found in X. Léon Dufour's "Bulletin d'exégèse du Nouveau Testament," *Rech. sc. rel.* 57 (1969) pp. 588-594 and I. Berten "Bulletin de Christologie protestante" *Rev. sc. phil. théol.* 55 (197), pp. 520-527.

8. W. Pannenberg, epilogue to I. Berten's book, *Histoire, révélation et foi.* Dialogue with Wolfhart Pannenberg, Brussels 1969, p. 112.

9. X. Léon-Dufour, *op. cit.*, 277.

10. H. Schleier, *La Résurrection de Jésus-Christ*, Mulhouse 1969, p. 43.

11. *Ibid.*, p. 47.

12. W. Pannenberg, *Jesus, God and Man*, Philadelphia 1968, pp. 53ff.

13. *Ibid.*

14. *Ibid.*, p. 69.

15. W. Pannenberg in "Historical and Theological Hermeneutics" in *Basic Questions in Theology* (p. 180, vol. I), quoted by I. Berten, *op. cit.*, p. 43. As an introduction to Pannenberg's theology of history I again recommend I. Berten's short book, *Histoire, révélation et foi.* Refer to chapter 4 of this book, pp. 63ff.

16. J. Moltmann, *Theology of Hope*, p. 84.

17. *Ibid.*, p. 20.

18. *Ibid.*, p. 21.

19. *Ibid.*, p. 88.